Praise for *Living in Freedom*

"For every woman of faith beset by tragic loss, for every believer whose devastating life experiences have ushered in spiritual struggles, and for the Christian who sometimes feels she has reached a dead end, *Living in Freedom* opens doors that once seemed closed, offering welcome spiritual direction for dealing with trauma and transition. With moving vignettes of real women suffering every imaginable adversity from sexual abuse through intimate partner violence to unspeakable grief of all kinds, the authors weave in solid biblical precepts and consistent invitations to prayerful reflection that can catalyze both healing and a recommitment to making life whole. This book pushes back against the darkness and points to the Light that is beckoning us all."

Robert A. Neimeyer, Ph.D.
Director, Portland Institute for Loss and Transition
Editor of *Techniques of Grief Therapy*

"In this life, pain isn't optional. No one is spared injury in this fallen world. This book will remind you that every woman you know lives with pain—and often unspeakable pain. The authors invite women to speak about their traumatic experiences, and their testimonies are powerful. There is pain, but there is also a biblical road map to living life with pain. It is a road of both healing and growth."

Dale Lunsford, Ph.D.
President, LeTourneau University

"All of us struggle with pain and difficulties in life, and too often we don't know where to turn for help. Tina has written a Bible-based, practical book that can help the reader climb out of the pit to a place of emotional and spiritual freedom. Tina uses her own story and the stories of other hurting women to remind us that we are not alone in our pain and to show us a path to healing."

Rayna Bomar
Attorney-at-Law

"Tina Elacqua has willingly, lovingly, and tenderly shared her journey of personal abuse and tragedy yet captures the essence of hope and freedom we have in Christ. Tina models for others how healing begins when someone comes out of hiding, tells her story, and realizes she is not alone in her pain and experience of injustice. This biblical road map is laced with Scripture and provides step-by-step directions and specific resources for a successful journey from surviving to thriving in Christ."

Pam Ramsey
Precepts International Bible Study Leader

"*Living in Freedom* is a powerful book that helps guide women through the aftermath of great trauma and toward Christ-centered healing. Using story after story, Tina

Elacqua invites the reader to wrestle with the reality of pain. As each woman uncovers her source of anguish, Tina bathes it in Truth. *Living in Freedom* gently leads women out of isolation and into the light of Jesus' gracious and merciful love. Tina helps readers remove the self-protective masks one by one, and then she slowly turns toward them the mirror so they can see the image of Christ appearing more and more clearly in their reflection. With her words, Tina creates a safe place for women to courageously choose greater trust in the Lord."

Amy Ragon
Director of Women's Ministry, Fellowship Bible Church

"Beautifully written and wonderfully edifying! The authors handle each woman's story with dignity and love as they delve into the tough questions they have for God during and after impossible situations. The biblical application and the exercises at the end of each chapter bring home ways to experience the healing and freedom that come from a personal relationship with Jesus Christ. It's a book you'll buy in multiples to hand out to friends. I know I will."

Jenny Smith
Writer

"*Living in Freedom* unlocks your pain, comes alongside you in your unfolding story, and draws you into a community of women who have experienced trauma. Honest words unfold, and painful truths are told. Yet these women not only survived their trauma, but they now flourish in their newfound freedom in Christ. Biblically based exercises end each chapter, creating a path for healing and hope as well as space for the Holy Spirit to heal your soul. Yes, healing and freedom in Christ are within your reach. Take the risk and journey with Jesus through this book."

June Hetzel, Ph.D.
Dean and Professor, School of Education, Biola University

"As Christian therapists, we walk daily with individuals who have suffered unspeakable harm, and we have learned that, even with the best psychotherapy and, at times, medication, there is no substitute for locking arms with someone who has been there. Dr. Elacqua invests in you with her expertise in trauma work, and she comes alongside you with her own story. Vulnerable about her own needs, healing, and hope, she is a fellow traveler on your journey."

Karen Pratt, APRN
Psychiatric Nurse Practitioner, Board Certified
Pepper Pratt, Ph.D.
LPC/MHSP, and author of *Hope for the Hurting* and *We're Just Talkin'*

"Dr. Elacqua has experienced great pain and has responded with even greater faith. If you have suffered tremendous anguish, this book will bless you with practical wisdom from God's Word and with inspiring examples of women who have learned that God's grace is sufficient for all things—even the most horrific situations. If your life journey has been a bit easier, this book will also bless you! All of us can benefit from the encouragement to walk in forgiveness, to live in spiritual abundance, and to rest in the grace of our incredibly loving Savior."

Jeannette Russ, Ph.D.
Professor of Engineering & Department Chair, Union University

"*Living in Freedom* is an enlightening view of trauma and tragedy from the perspective of survivors. But it's not just for survivors of trauma and abuse. This book is a tool that will equip you to support and encourage friends who have had trauma in their life."

Pam Means, LCSW
Author

"Dr. Elacqua provides a heartfelt step-by-step biblical process for facing and dealing with the inevitable pain caused by living in this sinful world. She describes the healing and freedom that stem from a close personal relationship with Jesus Christ. Dr. Elacqua is a testimony to God's healing and hope. *Living in Freedom* is a must-read. It will positively transform and inform your life."

Christine Gehman, LISW

"Wow! I wish I'd had this book 25 years ago! Dr. Elacqua not only knows deep personal pain and loss, but she has also experienced the life-transforming healing power of Jesus. Thank you, Tina, for not keeping the lessons you learned a secret. Thank you for instead writing a book that helps us learn how to face, overcome, and heal from past wounds so we can start *Living in Freedom*! A must-read for so many of the women I work with."

Gail Gustafson
Executive Director of the Dream Center

"Every human being knows pain, and sometimes their history keeps them from healing and living. The stories in this book help us know we are not alone or crazy or wrong to ask "Why?" and "Where was God?" This book demonstrates how Christians telling their stories and providing tools based on lessons they learned can help the hurting people as well as counselors working with clients. This book helps people who need to heal their memories feel understood, and it offers valuable, well-explained coping skills based on ancient and effective Christian practices. People who use this book on their journey are headed toward freedom."

Elizabeth Wilson, Ph.D., LCSW
Professor of Social Work, Union University

"Reader, take heart! You are not alone! *Living in Freedom* is a place where transformation happens. Its readers have moved from darkness into the light of Christ. What once held these women captive has been brought to the foot of the cross where true redemption happens. In the pages of this book, the authors share their own as well as other people's personal and painful stories. But the book does not stop there. The biblical framework for practical steps you can take provides a road map so you can experience the risen Savior and be empowered to walk in His grace and freedom."

Elaine Friedrich, Ph.D.
Director of Digital Discipleship, Mt. Bethel Church

"The interweaving of social research with personal stories by individuals who have experienced trauma gives *Living in Freedom* a special credibility. Also, rather than just telling readers that God can heal, the authors show women how they can partner with their Healer and find in Him the strength and courage to deal with the past as well as the future. The authors honor women by giving them a platform for sharing their pain as well as their victories, sharing that can't help but encourage readers."

Kelley Eltzroth
Professor of Psychology, Mid Michigan College

"*Living in Freedom* is a powerful book that supports women on their journey of overcoming trauma, abuse, loss, injustice, and other difficult life circumstances. Dr. Tina Elacqua eloquently narrates the practical, step-by-step application of Scripture that will help readers move toward empowerment, healing, and freedom. The life stories that supplement Dr. Elacqua's teaching resonate broadly as each contributor offers a very personal account of her specific experience. *Living in Freedom* is a treasure I will continue to reference to support my own mental and spiritual health when I encounter life's painful experiences."

Brandi Niemeier, Ph.D.
Associate Professor, Health Promotion, University of Wisconsin-Whitewater

"The heart-rending personal accounts in *Living in Freedom* remind us of the physical and emotional pain that is too often inflicted behind closed doors and then carried in that broken heart for years. Although hope often seems out of reach for individuals in dark places, this book reminds readers that available to them is supernatural power that can break the chains that hold back so many. *Living in Freedom* also offers readers step-by-step guidance for accessing life-transformative healing and courage in Christ."

Karen A. Longman
Professor and Ph.D. Program Director of Higher Education
Azusa Pacific University

LIVING IN

Freedom

A BIBLICAL ROAD MAP FOR NAVIGATING LIFE'S PAIN

Tina C. Elacqua, Ph.D.

WESTBOW
PRESS®
A DIVISION OF THOMAS NELSON
& ZONDERVAN

WestBow Press books may be ordered through booksellers or by contacting:

WestBow Press
A Division of Thomas Nelson & Zondervan
1663 Liberty Drive
Bloomington, IN 47403
www.westbowpress.com
844-714-3454

ISBN: 978-1-6642-0616-8 (sc)
ISBN: 978-1-6642-0615-1 (e)

Print information available on the last page.

WestBow Press rev. date: 10/27/2020

In my anguish I cried to the LORD,
and he answered by setting me free.
Psalm 118:5 (ERV)

DEDICATION

To fellow travelers on this journey of faith…

FOREWORD

From the moment we took our first breath, everything changed. The warm, quiet, tranquil security of our mother's womb disappeared in an instant. Our grand entrance was jarring, bright lights and loud voices were irritating, and people we didn't know were poking at us. Welcome to the world where pain and the unexpected can become the norm!

Life can be hard. Even from the onset. Those of us blessed to be raised by loving and emotionally healthy parents can generally grow into adulthood fairly unscathed, but for many others, that's not the case. Even in loving, safe homes, evil can slither its way into our lives, leaving us deeply wounded and not knowing whom we can truly trust.

We can spend an entire lifetime trying to stay ahead of our wounds, to hide from them, to bury them. What we don't realize is that when we bury them, we bury parts of ourselves, and when we do so, we aren't able to truly live life. You see, we were created for freedom. Trauma—regardless of how it presents itself in our lives— binds us. Still tethered to the pain, we limp through life. Oh, on the outside we can look put together and polished, but the inside tells a different story. The inside offers clear evidence that you and I can't bury our wounds. To one degree or another, your wounds will always bury you.

In Pursuit of Healing

As a Certified Domestic Violence Counselor and Marriage and Family Therapist for over 20 years, I have had the privilege of coming alongside fellow travelers who are trying to navigate life despite the trauma in their past—and every single one of them is a hero to me. Whenever we choose to pursue healing rather than allowing our wounds to become excuses, we change the trajectory of our life. By God's redemptive grace, dealing with our wounds can bring us to a healthier understanding of our value and our purpose in life. In God's hands, what could have destroyed us can be the very thing that drives us to tackle the challenging journey toward wholeness.

Counseling is one way we can pursue genuine healing and find real freedom from the wounds that bind us. This wonderful book offers another means of working through pain and moving toward freedom. Bravo to you for picking up *Living in Freedom*! Its wisdom and life-altering examples will definitely help you find your way.

Whatever means you choose to pursue healing and wholeness, know this all-important truth: you *can* heal—and heal well. Know, too, that your story matters. *You* matter. *Your freedom* matters. That said, healing that leads to authentic freedom will not knock on your door and invite itself into your life. You get to vote.

Remember when Jesus asked the man who had been paralyzed for 38 years, "Do you want to get well?" (John 5:6 NIV). Jesus could have healed the man immediately. Instead, Jesus first posed the question we all must answer: *Do we really want to be well?* Like the paralyzed man in that biblical story, we play an active role in our healing. Wrestling with this vital question is the first step we all must take. There are no shortcuts; there are no detours around it.

The Way to Healing

The book you hold in your hand is a precious and powerful gift. Page after page of *Living in Freedom* offers you an invitation to peek into the life of real people as they transparently share their real pain, their real stories, their real feelings, their real losses, and their very real choice to heal and live again. You will see that you are not alone.

Dr. Tina Elacqua is among the brave women who share their story. Writing about her experiences from a place of raw authenticity, Dr. Tina comes alongside you with truth that has the potential to change your life forever. This courageous woman offers something of a GPS that can help guide you to freedom, to a place of wholeness and health you may never have thought possible. Because Tina loves Jesus Christ and knows well the Word of God, she provides life-giving truths to guide you as you journey, one step at a time, away from your woundedness and pain.

There *is* a way to healing. That Way is the only Way that will truly set you free. That Way is named *Jesus*.

I encourage you to learn from Tina how to
follow Him to healing and wholeness,
to living in freedom!

Dr. Ramona Probasco holds a Doctorate in Psychology and has conducted extensive research in the area of domestic violence. She is a Marriage and Family Therapist, a Certified Domestic Violence Counselor, and a Nationally Certified Counselor. She has been in private practice for over twenty years. Dr. Ramona is an expert and sought-after speaker on domestic violence and how to authentically heal well from the trauma it causes. As a personal overcomer of domestic violence, she offers guidance and insight to others based on both her clinical expertise and her own experience of moving from victim to survivor to overcomer.

ACKNOWLEDGMENTS

First and foremost, I thank Jesus, my Lord and Savior. Without Him, I would never have been pulled from the pit and walking in freedom (Psalm 40:2).

My Lord brought Joy Greene and Jan Strickland into my life for a short but meaningful season. Together—and for God's kingdom—we developed the survey mentioned in this book and then began collecting data. At the time when life opportunities took them elsewhere, we had already gathered 400 responses.

The Lord then brought my beloved colleague at LeTourneau University, Dr. Vicki Sheafer, into my life as a dear friend, prayer partner, and researcher. With the help of our research assistants, Hannah Barnett and Miranda Lamb, and many friends and family members, we collected responses from over 1100 women! And without Vicki, I may have stopped this ministry project many years ago. She has been a consistent and faithful support.

The Lord knew that not just any professional editor would do. So He brought me Lisa Guest, a kindred spirit whose love and encouragement bless me beyond words.

The greatest gift my heavenly Father has given me, next to His Son, is Laird Jones. I am honored to be his wife. And it is a privilege to have Hannah Maria and Christina call me "Mama."

I am grateful to the more than 1100 women who completed the survey and/or shared their personal stories with me. They are compelling testimonies of God's transformative and healing power that enabled them to arrive at a place of freedom.

To you precious readers who are traveling this journey of faith, I am proud of you for taking these steps on the biblical road map for navigating life's pain. As you encounter more of Jesus, you will find freedom and peace. Stay true, my sister in Christ, to God's will for you—and know that His will for you truly is a life of freedom.

PREFACE

Precious one, I have been praying for you. Oh, I don't know you, and I may never have the privilege of meeting you and hearing you story. But I do know you have a story. A very important story. And I know that—like everyone's story—yours includes times of joy and times of sorrow....

In the pages of this book, several women tell their stories of loss and sorrow. What may make their stories different from yours is that these women are now living in freedom. They followed a biblical road map for navigating life's pain, and they found real freedom, the ability to truly live, abiding in Christ Jesus. I truly pray, that you will apply the strategies laid out in this book and, by God's grace, one day arrive at a place of peace and freedom. Hardly mysterious, these strategies are based on the truths found in God's Word, truths that have enabled many women—including me—to connect with Jesus and receive from Him healing for their heart.

As you read this book, you will:

- Grow in your faith and strengthen your walk with Jesus Christ
- Come to recognize the struggles women experience but rarely, if ever, share
- Realize you aren't the only person who has ever experienced certain circumstances or emotions
- Be encouraged by the truth that you are completely capable of doing what you need to do to know hope, comfort, and healing

- Receive practical and proven suggestions about how to daily cope with, survive, and even thrive despite experiences that wounded you and left their scars. These healing steps include nurturing a biblical faith, practicing spiritual disciplines, forgiving the people who caused you pain, learning to share your story, and relying on resources that are available in the church and community.
- Be equipped to walk through your own pain to a place of freedom from which you will minister to other hurting women

In addition, husbands will glean from these pages knowledge about how to better love their wives the way God intends them to. Brothers in the Lord will learn how to support their hurting sisters with the love of Christ. And pastors will gain insight that will help them more effectively counsel the women in their church.

Many women around the world are hurting, weighed down by longstanding wounds, shame, and fear. Many of these women consider themselves Christians, but they aren't yet living the abundant life Jesus longs for them to know (John 10:10). Instead, they are stuck in darkness. These sentences may even describe you....

My friend, I know tragedy, and I also know Jesus and the hope, the healing, and the freedom that only He can provide. I have experienced the healing power of Jesus and the peace that comes from knowing Him and studying His Word. Jesus, the Light of the world (John 8:12; 12:46), has shined into my darkness time and time again, teaching me about Himself and giving me insights that resulted in biblical strategies that encourage women to draw close to Jesus and allow Him to do His healing work. I hope you will give me the opportunity to journey with you. To pray for you as you read this book. To believe for you, if you don't believe it for yourself, that you also can arrive at this place of peace and live in freedom.

A BONUS GIFT FOR YOU

Being still before the Lord and meditating on His Word has been integral to my healing and my ability to live each day in freedom. That's why—and I hope this will be a blessing to you—I have created a PDF file of "God's Word for Life's Challenges." The list of scriptures chosen for each life challenge I address is suitable for framing.

To download your free "God's Word for Life's Challenges," please enter this address into your web browser.

http://doralcove.com/gods-word-for-lifes-challenges/

CONTENTS

INTRODUCTION

In the middle of the night on October 26, 2005, my parents were brutally murdered in their own home.

- On December 15, 2006, my baby, Rachel, left this temporary home called earth and met Jesus.
- My youngest, at age four, was diagnosed with autism spectrum disorder.
- As a child, I was abused.
- I grew up in a violent and alcoholic home until my courageous father—whom I lovingly called "Pop"—chose a life of freedom and sobriety.

As I struggled to figure out my life in the context of these horrific circumstances, I asked the Lord these hard questions:

"Am I all alone?" I found that I am like most people: we feel alone in our pain. We also often think—falsely—"I am the only person who has ever experienced this or felt like this."

"Am I losing it?" Like anyone and everyone else who has gone through hard times, I've experienced a myriad of emotions (grief, shock, anger, fear, shame) and numerous symptoms (anxiety, sleepless nights, headaches, depression, even suicidal thinking). In fact, my self-destructive feelings and symptoms were sometimes so intense that I found putting one foot in front of the other virtually impossible.

"Where are You?" Post-tragedy, I have often questioned where my ever-present God is. "What, God, are You doing to help me deal with this intense emotional pain?"

"Where were You?" And of course I have often questioned God and wondered where He was during the various painful and life-altering experiences I've faced. I have truly wondered how a loving and gracious Lord could allow these traumatic events. I asked God why He didn't step in and prevent the various incidents from happening.

"Will it ever end?" After one of life's storms subsides, I have often wondered—as most survivors do—whether I will ever be able to get over this experience, move on from this agonizing heartache, or be happy and whole again.

PAIN HAPPENS

I'm not alone. You're not alone. Far too many people have experienced inexcusable treatment, pain greater than they knew was even possible, sheer evil, and moments that no one should ever go through. Their homes have been filled with the unspeakable: domestic violence and/ or physical, sexual, emotional, and verbal abuse, arguments, fights, drug and alcohol addiction, a spouse's unfaithfulness, and/or the spouse's (or their own) addiction to pornography. Sometimes family members have terminal health issues, children have special needs, finances are tight, no support group is in place, and the demands of school, work, family, and even the church are overwhelming. Stress is compounded when a family deals with separation, divorce, remarrying, or blending families.

Of course, in all these and similarly agonizing circumstances, a person suffers mentally, physically, and emotionally. Anger, anxiety, worry, fear, and depression can be overwhelming. Some people try to stuff their feelings or find comfort or perhaps a sense of control over their chaotic life by over- or undereating, sometimes developing anorexia and bulimia. Other people experience a crisis of faith, either walking away from the Lord or questioning whether they ever truly knew Him. Some people do cling to Jesus Christ, holding on to their faith, allowing themselves to be molded into the image of Jesus.

Throughout the pages of this book, you'll hear the hearts of women as they speak with excruciating honesty about the deep pain they have known (see "The Women Who Spoke" on page xxv). You will also hear my heart and learn of the freedom I have found despite some horrific experiences and the dark days that followed. Our stories are not often told in polite company, much less in Christian circles. Yet these women and I have taken off our masks, those Christian façades that suggest all is well. What we have chosen to reveal is startling and heartbreaking, yet freedom and peace are available to every broken soul, to ours and to yours.

NOT ONLY SURVIVING ...

Despite their experiences, many of these courageous women are not merely surviving; they are thriving. And that's possible when, as wounded as we are, we respond to the invitation of Jesus Christ and begin to develop a personal and life-giving relationship with the Son of God who calls you and me "friend." In my journey, I found a community of believers who have endured tragedy yet are now thriving. I also found spiritual disciplines that ground me in the Word of God and thereby give me a foundation for

THE WOMEN WHO SPOKE

- *List three of the greatest struggles you have experienced.*
- *What helped you get through these struggles?*
- *What practical advice would you give to other women experiencing these same struggles?*

My research began with an online survey, comprised of these three questions, that I sent to Christian women across the nation, most of whom I had never met. These women, in turn, sent the survey to their Christian friends. Effort was made to ensure a sample that was large enough to be representative of the entire United States. I asked about marital status, ethnicity, age, city, state, if she were a Christian, and, if so, what denomination.

Women also had a chance to participate using paper-and-pencil surveys at Bible studies, conferences, and open houses. To ensure a wide range of ages, college students also had an opportunity to participate: two Christian universities made this survey available to the student body as well as to faculty and staff.

More than eleven hundred women responded, ranging in age from sixteen to eighty-nine. Most were married, with the second largest group being single; then, divorced/separated; and, the smallest group, widowed. More than half of the respondents were white. Most of the fifty states were represented, and the respondents were affiliated with almost fifty different Christian denominations.

These precious women poured out their hearts as they shared their most intimate struggles. Many of them added a personal note of appreciation and expressed their willingness to tell more of their story. Finally, someone was listening.

making choices according to His plan for His children.

But what have others done to thrive? What helped these women endure the pain in the moment as well as throughout the long aftermath? What works? What doesn't work? How did they come to flourish after the storm calmed? What enables them to continue flourishing? I am also interested in why some women walk away from the Lord, why others hold on to their faith, and—remarkably—how women who did not know the Lord, find Jesus in the midst of the darkness. Interestingly, as they identified specific methods of enduring the pain and eventually thriving, I realized that the women I mention are quite similar to me. And, I'm guessing, to you. They describe helpful practices and offer compassionate advice to other women dealing with pain caused by unspeakable trauma.

I have great respect for the brave women who shared their experiences here and great hope for readers who have yet to step into the light of healing and freedom—and you may be one of them. That's why I'm dedicating this book to fellow survivors, to readers who identify with the women who share their stories in this book. Able to relate to these accounts as if they were their very own stories, these precious women may find a real heart connection with the courageous women who, on these pages, have spoken with transparency and genuineness. Ideally, the women you meet here will inspire and motivate you to bring your own secrets out of the darkness and into the light where healing can begin.

As you read this book, I know that you will gain tools that will help you thrive despite life's pain and that, in time, God will enable you to come alongside a wounded woman as she walks toward the only Hope there is in this fallen world: Jesus Christ.

The Lord bless you, my friend,
Tina

PART
ONE

*You're Not
Alone*

CHAPTER **ONE**

Coming Out of Hiding

"IT'S OUR LITTLE SECRET"—those four words may send chills down your spine. That simple statement can hold a person in chains for years, for decades. This very wrong kind of secret erodes trust and confidence, breaks hearts and relationships, and destroys hopes and dreams. This kind of secret can lead to—among other things—self-hatred, self-harm, and struggles with physical intimacy in a marriage. Being told to keep sexual abuse a secret can sentence a soul to prison....

And maybe you know far too well what I'm talking about. I'm going to share Christie's story right now, and it may be similar to yours. Or maybe one of this chapter's other accounts—about child abuse, sexual molestation, rape, incest, pornography, or domestic violence—reflects your experience. I share the stories in this first chapter to do more than offer real-life examples and occasionally some general information; I share these stories so that you just might find a kindred spirit... and some hope. First, Christie's story....

> But he's supposed to love me... He's supposed to be taking care of me... Why is he doing this? Why does he keep hurting me like this?

Whenever I lay there, being treated like a piece of property he used for his sexual pleasure and fulfillment, I felt dirty, defiled, and contaminated. I also felt confused about why this supposed-to-be protector and caregiver repeatedly did to me what was so strange and so hurtful.

The abuse continued for many years. It was not until circumstances in his life took him out of my life that the abuse stopped. At least abuse by him.

One day—I think I was fifteen—I was arguing and physically fighting with a family member. I don't even remember what we were arguing about. We often fought, but this time the argument was different because I was different. I had had enough. I'd come to terms with the rage I felt toward her. I was furious that she had allowed the abuse to happen. I had always seen her as a protector, yet she hadn't protected me. Instead, for all those years, she had allowed the abuse to happen—and I could no longer contain the rage.

I remember the exact place I was standing—in the dining room, close to the entrance of the family room. And I remember yelling, "Why weren't you there for me when [my perpetrator] sexually abused me?"

She stopped dead in her tracks and pulled back on the blow I was about to receive. She said, "What?"

As soon as the words came out of my mouth, I wanted to stuff them back in. In a shaky, scared voice, I said, "I'm not supposed to tell. It's our little secret."

But she said, "No! You must tell me."

I found the courage, and I told her.

I was amazed at how brief my story was, but I was glad that the issue would now be taken care of. Once and for all, justice would be served. That's what I thought at the time, but that's not at all what happened.... I experienced humiliation and condemnation instead of compassion and empathy. Clearly, the theme was "Get over it!" There were few exceptions to this devastating response.

But I did not get over it. I could not get over it. How do you get over being sexually and emotionally abused? Through time, counseling, and a relationship with Jesus Christ, I learned that survivors of sexual abuse simply do not get over it. What they do is learn to live in freedom despite what has been done to them. Friend, this process of learning to walk in freedom begins with the biblical step of choosing to be courageous and tell the secret. We expose what was done in darkness and bring it into the light (Ephesians 5:11).

If you're thinking it's a little difficult to step out of an abusive, chaotic world physically and then emotionally and psychologically, you're right. That step—as well as the steps that follow—will always take courage, and the beautifully, painfully transparent stories at the heart of this book reflect each woman's remarkable courage. These precious women bravely shared their stories and revealed their brokenness, heartache, and pain as well as their resiliency and the hope they placed in the only Source of real hope, Jesus Christ.

Again, you may have a long-kept secret. If so, I hope this chapter inspires you to share your hidden secret with someone safe. Talking about your experience of child sexual abuse, molestation, rape, pornography, domestic violence, and/or something else will bring it into the light where healing can start.

CHILD SEXUAL ABUSE: MOLESTATION AND RAPE

Women like Christie and me are not at all alone in our experience of child sexual abuse. Did you know that one in five girls and one in twenty boys are victims of child sexual abuse? The National Center for Victims of Crime reports that 20 percent of adult females and 5 to

10 percent of adult males recall a childhood sexual assault or sexual abuse incident. Maybe you are one of these individuals. Experts agree, however, that the actual occurrence of child sexual abuse is difficult to determine. It is often not reported when the abused person is a child, and she may not come forward for years or decades, if ever. Maybe you are among this group. Maybe you understand all too well how hard and sometimes even how dangerous it is to report the abuse to a trusted family member (if there even is one), much less to a government organization.

Sometimes, though, we who have been abused are silent because we have no one to turn to. You see, in the majority of cases, the perpetrator of sexual abuse is someone we love and trust, someone who usually has significant power over us. As one woman shared, finding out about her daughter's sexual abuse stirred up memories of her own experiences and of the people closest to her whom she never told. She wrote, "Finding out that my daughter had been molested and kept it a secret for almost a year—that made me come to terms, yet again, with my own molestation that my parents, still to this day, know nothing about. And it's been my secret going on twenty-two years."

Such secrets about incidents of molestation—as well as rape and incest—are held in silence by people raised in both non-Christian homes and Christian homes. One woman shared, "When she was ten, my daughter was molested in our home by a babysitter from our [Christian church] youth group." Another woman wrote that her greatest struggle in dealing with her sexual abuse is that a minister was one of the guilty parties.

Even if adults haven't experienced sexual abuse themselves, they can understand why shame, fear, and loyalty will keep children from telling anyone about what has happened. Furthermore, children often conclude that what happened to them is their fault. Sometimes the perpetrator told them so, and other times the conclusion that they're bad is not as frightening as concluding that the perpetrators—who may be their own parents—are bad. Children may also think their loved ones will be hurt if they reveal who is abusing them: children too often swallow this lie that the perpetrator feeds them.

Another complicating factor is the reality that the perpetrator is often someone who plays a positive role in the child's life. For example, as one woman stated, "the abuser was the main person who made time to play games, who built snowmen and igloos with me, who helped me memorize my multiplication facts, and who recorded the hours I wore my retainer. I trusted him and he was fun (most times) to spend time with." The fact that the abuser is usually not all bad makes the abuse even more confusing for the child and further reduces the likelihood of her telling anyone who might help.

The child finds herself even more confused—and the situation is more complicated—when those she loves are the offenders or are to some degree allowing the abuse to occur. One woman shared her deep pain: "During the time that my mom lost her mind, I was sexually molested because my mother was crazy and arranged the whole thing." Another woman told me that her alcoholic mother forced her to marry the mother's alcoholic boyfriend. Later, after he robbed a store and was caught, this woman was able to have the marriage annulled. Countless women have told me that the men in their life (father, stepfather, brother, uncle, mother's boyfriend, etc.) sexually abused them even when Mom was close by and well aware, but chose to look the other way.

Not surprisingly, the trauma these sexually abused women—and men—experience can lead to mental health issues such as post-traumatic stress disorder (PTSD), depression, suicide, drug and alcohol abuse, low self-esteem, mistrust, and generalized anxiety disorder. One woman had a thirty-two-year battle with depression resulting from her sexual abuse. Another woman spoke of "dealing with the psychological and emotional aftermath of discovering that my daughter had been sexually assaulted by a boy her same age. I believe the aftermath has continued until this day—and she is now thirty years old." I also see depression in many of the women living at the homeless shelter, where I have volunteered. The majority of these residents are survivors of sexual abuse.

One woman had much to say about the sexual abuse done to her by her biological father and how this trauma led her down a path of shame, low self-esteem, alcohol abuse, and further sexual abuse:

I was raised in a Christian home and don't remember a time when I didn't believe in God. I accepted Jesus Christ as my Savior when I was seven. When I was growing up, we went to church every Sunday, but our parents had deep relationship issues that had a really negative effect on our family. My mom was struggling with postpartum depression, and she pushed my dad away sexually. In turn, he looked to my two sisters and me for sexual gratification [not intercourse]. Eventually he confessed to everything, and we forgave him.

I think this abuse really affected my view of myself. I never felt that I was worthy of love, and I had a very negative self-image. God always blessed me with lots of friends, but I always felt terribly lonely inside. I felt I had to carry this secret about my dad all on my own. I didn't look to my Savior for healing and comfort. Again, I thought I had to carry it all myself. When I turned twenty-one, I started going to bars and getting drunk. For the first time ever, I experienced release from all the pain and heartache. I loved drinking.

In a matter of months, I went home with a guy and lost my virginity. I felt so ashamed afterward. I didn't want anyone to know because all my single friends were virgins. I continued to hide my party lifestyle from my friends and family. I found myself in some very bad situations, and I was raped twice. These experiences all led to more shame and more keeping secrets from people.

After about a year and a half, I knew I couldn't live like this anymore. God started to change my heart. I prayed every single day that He would change me and use me for good for Him. I was sick of letting myself be used by men. I started getting counseling and was so humbled by my counselor's response. No matter what I shared about my past and about my current struggles, she would say—every time—"Do you know, Jesus still loves you so much?"

Remembering all the pain I bore unnecessarily brings tears to my eyes. I had an Advocate who had already voluntarily carried my guilt—as well as the guilt of those who had hurt me—to the cross. Turning my life around was not easy. Breaking those harmful party habits wasn't easy, but God provided me with the strength to quit that lifestyle and to apologize to my close friends and family, the people I had lied to about my partying. I lost friends in the process, but I take great comfort in the One who loves me unconditionally: Jesus Christ.

I am faithfully married now, and we are expecting our third baby. My relationship with my dad is incredible. My heart belongs to my Savior. I know that I can trust Him to help me resist any temptation now, and that gives me genuine confidence. He is mine, and I am His.

Another woman acknowledged a similar experience: "Throughout my entire life, I have dealt with diagnosed anxiety and depression as a result of sexual abuse as a child, which was not validated by my parents until my adolescent years. This has caused me great emotional pain, and my struggles continue in the present in my daily life." As many women battling depression realize, keeping secrets stashed away in the dark takes its toll.

PORNOGRAPHY

Despite what you may have heard—or, sadly, you may know this fact because of your own experience—pornography is not only a male problem. Pornography is an addiction that both men and women battle. Like their male counterparts, many women with an addiction to pornography find it tough to maintain sexual integrity when they're on the internet.

A Christian friend of mine has struggled with pornography since she was quite young, and she told her husband before they were married. He didn't admit his own struggle with pornography until just recently, after more than twenty years of marriage. This friend, now in her fifties, has only recently found freedom from pornography. Her Christian husband, however, has yet to do the same. In fact, he even denies that it's a problem.

As my friend talked about the negative effects of pornography on a marriage, I realized how significantly pornography negatively influences a husband's view of his wife. He sees her not as a co-heir in Christ, but as an object for his sexual gratification. Instead of viewing her as his equal, he sees her as his servant, a slave who will cook, clean, and take care of him and their children. Her husband always persuades her to put his sexual needs, desires, wants, and whims above her own because—as he often tells her—he is the most important member of the family. Perhaps you have experienced this firsthand.

One woman reflected at length about how her own addiction to pornography has affected her:

> I have struggled with my weight and my self-image most of my life since puberty. As a result, I was very easy prey to internet predators who used flattery to troll for vulnerable girls who would engage in sexual conversations. Through that, an appetite was awakened, and it evolved into my involvement with internet pornography. Even though I was thankfully spared from the men who tried to use me, I was not spared from the lure of those images. I am still trying to undo what they did to my sense of womanhood and to my ideas about the value of women in general. I

❦ TINA C. ELACQUA, PH.D. ❧

found that even though I am a woman, I was looking down on women as a whole and seeing all of us as objects.

I didn't even realize I had that view until I was married and noticed the degree of my self-loathing in many situations, both intimate and everyday. I had continued to struggle off and on with the porn and magazine images even though I was a Christian. I knew it was wrong, and God was very clear, telling me that He did not want me hurting myself that way. But, sadly, I continued to give in to the lure, and then I'd loathe myself even more.

It wasn't until I started opening up to other women—who were women of God—and sharing honestly about my struggles that I was able to see the truth of the problems and the lies I was believing. I can honestly say, I have been free of viewing sites that are bad for anyone to see, and I have a better perspective on myself and on women in general. Still, the battle is a daily one, but when I take a moment to quiet myself and talk to God, He is always there to remind me how much He loves me.

Whether a man or a woman is addicted to pornography, the destructive effects reach beyond the addict. For years, one woman dealt with the aftermath of her former husband who, when they were married, had struggled with porn and been unfaithful. Consider the fact that every view of a pornographic image is adultery: it is a sexual connection with someone outside the bonds of marriage. And as many women said in their responses to the survey, pornography leads to a lack of sexual satisfaction in their own marriage and a lack of sexual desire for the spouse the Lord has given them. Again, this experience may—sadly—be yours.

DOMESTIC VIOLENCE

Another secret that many women hide is the violence that occurred or is occurring in their own family: these women are hurt by those they love. The National Domestic Violence Hotline defines *abuse* as "a repetitive pattern of behaviors to maintain power and control over an intimate partner. These are behaviors that physically harm, arouse fear, and prevent a partner from doing what they wish or forcing them to behave in ways they do not want." (Yet every abuser I've met has blamed the victim for the abuse. All abusers blame those they hit: "They asked for it!")

In heartbreaking words, some women admitted that when they married a Christian man, they wrongly believed that domestic violence would never be an issue. (You too?) One woman "married who I thought was a Christian man, but he hit me and divorced me for a woman he was having an affair with." And, sadly, she is hardly alone. Many women struggle with the discovery and aftermath of their husbands' adulterous affairs. Tragically, when these precious women ask the church for help, they are often blamed for the situation and hear appalling comments like these:

- "God is sovereign, and He is allowing this for a reason."
- "Why did you put up with this for so many years?"
- "You must have asked for it!"
- "The Bible tells us to submit."

Clearly, we the church need to respond with wisdom, grace, and practical help. These women can feel very much alone and often frightened, as you yourself may know all too well.

Women who have experienced domestic violence are also quite vulnerable to the frequent invitation to return to their dangerous but familiar situation. Most abusers promise never to hurt them again, and for a short—very short—time, they don't. Eventually, however, the abusive cycle comes full circle: violence returns, then comes an apology, and a short time of peace exists... until the next burst of violence. One woman who was the target of mental, physical, and verbal abuse said, "I was repeatedly promised, 'I will never do that again.' At first, I chose to believe him. However, I came to realize that unless he received professional help, he was never going to change. I chose to not wait to find out what the outcome would be."

Research into the leading outcomes of domestic violence suggests that this woman's situation would have ended in either her death at the hands of her abuser, her suicide, or homelessness. That said, a safe home for women and children is a life-saving alternative, and one may be located closer to you than you think. Your church or the internet may be able to help you find one. If you are experiencing domestic violence, leave immediately. Your safety and, if you're a mother, your children's safety are paramount.

Occasionally, however, it is our children rather than our husbands who are guilty of violent assault in the home. A friend of mine adopted a young girl who later abused my friend—the adoptive mother— physically, emotionally, and verbally. This child's early years of living with her biological single mother were filled with violence and sexual abuse, and she chose to continue to act violently as a teenager and now as an adult. With counseling and the Lord's healing, she could have learned a new way of life. Instead, by court order, she is no longer allowed to live under the same roof as her adoptive parents. Domestic violence is never something to be tolerated or kept secret. Too much—your very life—is at stake.

SOURCES OF PAIN

As I mentioned in the introduction, over eleven hundred women wrote honestly, openly, and anonymously about themselves and their struggles. They provided specific information about the sources of their personal pain and about what helped them endure and, later, even thrive despite their losses. Although these women represent great diversity in age and faith, they all survived dreadful circumstances.

Perhaps the source of your pain is not described above. If that's the case, you may be able to identify with one or more of these struggles:

- Christian women and/or their loved ones are struggling to stand strong against—or, worse, are giving in to—drug and alcohol abuse.
- Some women have experienced their spouse's unfaithfulness or have themselves been unfaithful, resulting in a long-term affair, a series of affairs, and/or an addiction to pornography.
- We can be surprised by the intensity of our grief over the loss of loved ones—a child, spouse, parent, close friend, or family member.
- The daily responsibilities of caring for elderly parents can be exhausting and sometimes lonely.
- Prejudice and discrimination at work can be painful and even harmful.
- Anger, anxiety, worry, fear, and depression take a toll on one's mental, physical, and emotional health.
- Some women try to stifle their pain by over- or undereating: obesity, anorexia, or bulimia becomes a daily struggle.
- Children have special needs, and/or family members are dealing with life-threatening health issues.
- The stress of life is compounded by separation, divorce, remarriage, and blended families.
- Some women lack finances, social support, and time to take good care of themselves.
- School, work, children, family, and church activities can make life feel overwhelming.

Precious one, no words can fully express the agony of what some of you have experienced. Too many paths lead to a heartache that is actually a physical pain; to despair that can call into question long-held foundational truths; and to mental and emotional anguish that seems inescapable. The options listed above are among those paths. Which path is yours? Please don't end this chapter without identifying the sources of your pain. That is the first step to biblical freedom: you must come out of hiding and bring into the light all that has caused you pain.

THOUGHTS FROM A FELLOW TRAVELER

Having experienced many of the short- and long-term destructive effects of keeping our dark secrets hidden, I know that doing so is not God's will for us. Dear one, God desires authenticity in our inward being. He wants you to be fully transparent and real with Him. Granted, He knows your inward thoughts and what you're feeling. But—trust me—it is life-changing to say those thoughts and feelings out loud to your loving Creator.

Whether you have been forced against your will to take part in any immoral activities or if you participated in any by choice, please know you can find comfort and healing in Jesus Christ. Know, too, that— as you have seen in the words of women who are no longer hiding their secrets—you are not alone. I, too, have survived some terrible situations and can offer empathy, compassion, and some hard-won wisdom as I come alongside you in this journey. You are a survivor, and God desires to heal you. He wants you to walk in freedom from your heartaches, your past traumas, and their repercussions.

Please know that the child abuse, sexual molestation, rape, incest, or domestic violence you have experienced is *not* your fault. Regardless of what you have been told, you did *not* ask for it. No one asks to be beaten or raped or molested. The responsibility for the sinful acts and the damage done rests solely on the abuser, and he or she will definitely know the Lord's judgment.

Now, what about you? You have the opportunity to choose to move forward in the healing process. My beloved sister, hear me: God desires to heal you, and He is able to heal you, but whether you allow God to do that work in you is your choice. Making the choice to pursue healing and freedom will be difficult. Saying yes to God's invitation to heal you requires courage as well as the willingness to sit in the ashes and process with Jesus Christ the pain you have endured for far too long.

I know that not everyone desires or even feels able to move forward, and maybe that's you. Keeping secrets hidden and suppressing feelings and pain are familiar ways of coping and leaving the familiar—however hurtful and damaging that familiar is—can be hard. Too many of us women choose to sweep our feelings under the rug in hopes it will never be lifted and they will never be revealed. Precious one, the rug will be lifted at some point, if not by you voluntarily, then by daily events of life. Such events are called triggers. Someone will say or do something, you'll have a strange sense of déjà vu, or you'll hear a certain song, and that trigger will remind you of—or make all too real—the pain of those past experiences. Furthermore, unaddressed, your pain from the past will keep you from truly living in the freedom God wants you to have in the present and the future. So I pray that you will choose to face right now what you need to face. Know that God's Holy Spirit, who lives in you if you have named Jesus as your Savior and Lord, will give you the courage and strength you need for this difficult but essential work.

Now, I do understand that not everyone who has picked up a copy of this book is a believer. Whether you desire to know Jesus Christ for the first time or to recommit your life to Him, you will find the sidebar "An Invitation to Know Christ" helpful (page 16). May you truly recognize how much God loves you and what an amazing gift He is offering you in His Son, Jesus.

PERSONAL REFLECTION AND APPLICATION

I do hope you'll use this book to learn more about Jesus, your good Shepherd who desires to walk with you in the ups and downs of life. He is close to the brokenhearted, and He saves those who are crushed in spirit (Psalm 34:18). He will comfort you with His presence, and He will bring healing to the wounds you have experienced in this fallen world.

As you read this book, take time to think about the Personal Reflection and Application questions that close every chapter. I also encourage you to gather with a small group of friends—women like you who are willing to be transparent and genuine—to discuss the questions. Pray for and encourage one another as you journey together toward the healing and the freedom God has for you.

1. Dear friend, I'm truly thrilled that you picked up this book and are willing to allow the Lord to speak to your broken heart. Before you go on to chapter 2, ask the Lord what He wants for you as you read those pages. What are you asking God to do in you as you go through the content presented there? Take time now and write a short prayer: share with the Lord your specific desires for how He will speak to you and heal you.

2. Which of the hidden secrets discussed in this chapter do you most identify with? Explain. If none of these secrets are yours, what painful experience do you want to bring into the light?

3. On several index cards or sticky notes, write part or all of this statement: "I am beautiful, valued, and loved by God. In Christ, I am free. I am NOT guilty. I have been rescued, saved, restored, and repaired. I am a new creature in Christ." Put these notes to yourself in places where a reminder would be helpful. Every time you see it, acknowledge the truth of what you read. Also, I encourage you to say all of these facts aloud—and with growing confidence—ten times a day.

PRAYER: *Lord Jesus, thank You for being close to the brokenhearted, for being close to me in my pain. You know I am grieving hidden secrets about things done to me and/or to those I love. I have believed lies fed to me by Satan and/or by the world, I've acted on those beliefs for too long, and now I struggle to accept the truth about Your love and Your healing power. Help me to live in a right relationship with You. Help me know the Bible and follow the blueprint for life that You have given me in its pages.*

An Invitation to Know Christ

We are all sinners.
All have sinned and fall short of the glory of God. Romans 3:23
Not a single person can claim to have led a perfect life and never sinned. We fail to live up to our own standards, and of course we fail to live up to God's.

Sin separates us from God.
The wages of sin is death, but the free gift of God is eternal life in Christ Jesus our Lord. Romans 6:23
The consequence of our sin is death. As a result of sin, we all experience physical death. Some will also experience spiritual death, which is separation from God that lasts for all eternity. People who choose to reject God throughout their earthly life will experience forever their choice to live apart from God: this separation is called hell.

God provides a way for us sinners to have a relationship with Him.
"God so loved the world that he gave his only Son, so that everyone who believes in him may not perish but may have eternal life." John 3:16
God proves his love for us in that while we still were sinners Christ died for us. Romans 5:8
God is a God of justice and a God of mercy. The death of His sinless Son, Jesus Christ, was the perfect, complete, once-and-for-all sacrifice for the sins of humanity. Jesus' spilled blood paid the required price for our sins, and His death enabled God to show us the mercy of forgiveness, the grace of being

References

"Abuse Defined" at The National Domestic Violence Hotline, 2011, accessed April 6, 2018, http://www.thehotline.org/is-this-abuse/abuse-defined/#tab-id-6.

"Child Sexual Abuse Statistics" at The National Center for Victims of Crime, 2012, accessed April 6, 2018, https://www.victimsofcrime.org/media/reporting-on-child-sexual-abuse/child-sexual-abuse-statistics.

~ TINA C. ELACQUA, PH.D. ~

BIBLICAL TRUTH INSPIRES US TO EXPOSE DARKNESS

Take no part in the unfruitful works of darkness, but instead expose them. For it is shameful even to mention what such people do secretly; but everything exposed by the light becomes visible, for everything that becomes visible is light. Therefore it says,

> *"Sleeper, awake!*
> *Rise from the dead,*
> *and Christ will shine on you."*

Be careful then how you live, not as unwise people but as wise, making the most of the time, because the days are evil. So do not be foolish, but understand what the will of the Lord is. — Ephesians 5:11-17

Dear one, the will of the Lord is for you to expose the darkness, tell the secret, and ask for help.

Hotline Resources

If you're thinking about taking your life, please call the **National Suicide Prevention Lifeline** at 1-800-273-8255. Or call 911. God loves you more than you can grasp, and He doesn't want you to live with that

in relationship with Him, and the hope of spending eternity with Him in His glorious heaven.

Our salvation is by God's grace alone. *By grace you have been saved through faith, and this is not your own doing; it is the gift of God—not the result of works, so that no one may boast.* Ephesians 2:8-9 No one can earn forgiveness, a relationship with a holy God, or eternal life in heaven. Each of those is an aspect of God's gracious gift of salvation. When we recognize that Jesus died to pay the price for our sins and that He did so for no other reason except His love for us, we can choose to receive that gift of spiritual life now and for eternity. Will you receive it?

Confess your sin, ask Jesus' forgiveness, and live with Him as Lord of your life. *Everyone who calls on the name of the Lord shall be saved.* Romans 10:13 *If you confess with your lips that Jesus is Lord and believe in your heart that God raised him from the dead, you will be saved. For one believes with the heart and so is justified, and one confesses with the mouth and so is saved.* Romans 10:9-10 God loves you so much that He was willing to let His own Son die, but God raised Jesus from the dead. Choosing to believe this truth is choosing relationship with God. We respond to His love with our love and obedience: we respond by living with Jesus as our Lord and as the reason for everything we do.

Are you ready to accept the invitation? If you are ready to have a relationship with God, made possible by the death and resurrection of Jesus, simply pray as follows:

Dear God, I am a sinner, imperfect and struggling. I acknowledge You as God, holy and completely free of sin. I come to You for forgiveness, grateful for the sacrificial gift of Your Son, Jesus, who died as payment for my sins. Thank You for saving my soul from eternal separation from You, and I am choosing to name Jesus my Savior and Lord. In response to Your love, I want to live a life that honors You in every way. Come into my life to reign, to teach me, and to lead me. And please enable me to both receive Your love and to love You well. Amen.

Growing in Your Faith

- God did not design us to journey through life alone. We are to be active in a community of fellow believers where we get solid biblical teaching and meet people who will care for us, pray for us, and love us. This community is a Bible-believing church.

- Every day, make some time to read God's Word. The New Testament book of Mark or Luke—each is an account of Jesus' life—is a good place to start. And if you're able to join a Bible study, do!

- Talk to God. That's what praying is: talking to the Lord as openly as you would talk with a friend.

Please let me know (www.doralcove. com) of your decision to recommit your life to Jesus or to—for the first time— accept Him as your Savior and invite Him to be your Lord.

intense pain—and He doesn't want you to take your life.

Beloved, if you are being abused, know that God does not want you to be treated like that. Please call the **National Domestic Violence Hotline** at 1-800-799-SAFE (7233) or 1-800-787-3224 (TTY). And use this website to develop a Safety Plan with your trained domestic violence counselor:

https://drramona.com/safety-plans/

It is not God's will for you to be sexually assaulted. If you have been, please call **The Rape, Abuse, and Incest National Network** at 1-800-656-HOPE (4673).

If you are dealing with the destructive effects of pornography, please call the **National Victim Assistance Helpline** at 1-800-583-2964.

You are God's precious child. Please reach out for help and allow the Lord to heal your pain, transform your life, and enable you to live in freedom. I know He can do it because… He has done it for me.

CHAPTER **TWO**

Shining God's Light in the Darkness

AS I STATED IN the first chapter, *this process of learning to walk in freedom begins with the biblical step of choosing to be courageous and tell the secret.* Precious one, you must come out of hiding and share with safe, trustworthy sisters the darkness you have experienced. Then, open your heart to step 2 and *let God shine His light into your darkness.*

Allow me to share some of my dear friend Emily's story. It will help you to see the importance of exposing the darkness by inviting God to shine His light:

> *It all started with my feeling tired. I noticed I had no energy. Gradually, over the course of time, I also noticed a growing sense of fear and anxiety, of judgment and failure. I began rapidly losing weight not because I was trying to, but because I completely lost my appetite. And nothing in life was enjoyable anymore. It was becoming more and more difficult to get out of bed.*

I didn't want to see anyone or talk to anyone. My thoughts became more and more negative. I felt like a fraud. I was a house of cards waiting to tumble down. It finally dawned on me that I—a psychologist and professor—was depressed. That realization—that truth—felt like one more failure to add to the list. Right up there with "Christians aren't supposed to suffer from mental illness. They should just pray harder and have more faith." Great, so now I'm a horrible Christian and a psychologist with a mental disorder who is supposed to be teaching and training the next generation.

I started going to counseling. I also started taking various antidepressants and anti-anxiety medications. They never helped very much. The side effects were always worse than any benefit I received. I tried at least six different kinds of medications. After a while, I was told that I had medication-resistant depression. I was a medication failure as well.

Christmastime came and went. I was not ready to start teaching a new semester. I tried to start, but I was growing increasingly suicidal. I had lost all hope. My mind was a swirling vortex of self-hatred, shame, and guilt. I couldn't do anything right. I was letting everybody down. No one loved me, not even God. Twenty-four hours a day, day after day, mental torment was the only constant. I began to think about swallowing all the pills in all those bottles. My counselor and I made the decision that I needed to go to the hospital. I stayed four days. I should have stayed longer, but instead of getting the help I needed, I said all the right things and got myself out of the hospital.

I began to stay in bed more days than not. I wasn't sleeping, and I couldn't leave the house. One of the days I actually managed to make it to school, I was told I was placed on medical leave. In hindsight, I see that the school's decision put me on the right path, but at the time their decision felt like a death sentence. I now had no job and no hope. I had failed at everything. I was a colossal disappointment to myself, the world, and the Lord.

My counselor found a program for me. I didn't say much the first few days. I was too ashamed. I didn't want people to know that I was a Christian, and I certainly didn't want them to know that I was a psychologist. My days consisted of several group therapy sessions and an individual session. The group was made up of all kinds of people with all kinds of mental health issues. We had people with depression, addictions, bipolar, and generalized anxiety disorder.

One day we were all outside on break. A young man who was battling addiction problems asked me what I did for a living. It was the moment I had dreaded. I tried to deflect the question by saying I was a college professor. When he asked what I taught, I thought about lying and saying I taught math. I figured no one would ask any more questions about that, but on the off chance that he did (I don't know much about math), I just said psychology. I expected him to start laughing and ask me why a psychologist was in the nut house. But that's not at all what happened. Instead of this being my biggest moment of shame, the Lord used this moment to begin my journey back to health. This young man told everyone in the group to be quiet. When all eyes were on him, he said, "Hey, everybody! Emily is a psychology professor. Isn't that awesome?"

That's when the Lord spoke to my heart. I had felt like Peter after he denied the Lord three times. I thought my life and my service to the Lord were done. I felt disqualified, too broken to be used. But just as the Lord restored Peter (John 21:15-19), He restored me. My fellow patients started calling me "Doc." They asked me questions about their illness, about their relationships, about their treatment. When they found out that I taught at a Christian university, they asked me to pray for them and for their families.

My healing was not instantaneous. I still had a lot of hard work ahead of me. I remained in counseling for another year. The Lord was faithful and is faithful. That was almost twenty years ago. I haven't had another episode of depression. I was restored to my job, my family, my friends, my ministry. I have great compassion for those who suffer from mental illness, a degree of compassion that I didn't have before. I also hope I'm less judgmental than I used to be.

God healed me, He restored me, and He carries me day by day. He truly is my Redeemer King.

JESUS IS THE LIGHT

As we saw in Emily's story, she took the first step toward living in freedom when she came out of hiding. She acknowledged before God and others that she was depressed, struggling with self-condemnation, and haunted by suicidal thoughts. Jesus worked on Emily's behalf, but she didn't see His hand in her life at first. When Emily was placed on medical leave, she said it felt like a death sentence. In hindsight, however, she was able to see the decision as Jesus' way of placing her on the path toward living in freedom.

As Emily continued to expose the darkness in her life and her soul, God continued to shine His light. He spoke to her heart through His Word, through fellow patients at the mental institution, and through professional Christian counseling. The darkness did not instantaneously go away, as is expected. Yet Emily kept taking the steps she needed to take in order to one day walk in freedom.

If Emily had failed to identify and bring into the light the source of her pain as well as its ongoing impact on her, she would not be where she is today…thriving in her role as a child of God who is serving His people. Also, God used Emily's time of walking in the darkness, of living with despair and hopelessness, to mold her character: God made Emily more like His Son, her Redeemer: more compassionate, more understanding, and less judgmental. The Lord used this dark season to make Emily a better psychologist and to increase her ability to minister to people in need.

Precious one, if you have not yet responded to my chapter 1 encouragement to identify the source of your pain, won't you do so now? Ask God to help you bring your darkness into His light. Ask Jesus—who is the Light of the World—to shine His light on your darkest pain so that you can follow Him to healing, wholeness, and redemption just as Emily did (John 8:12, 12:46; Ephesians 5:11).

SITTING IN THE ASHES

No one would ever choose pain over peace. Yet it is in our darkest, most pain-filled moments that God molds us more into the image of Jesus. When I reflect on my life, it was when I was willing to sit in my ashes of despair, hopelessness, and pain that God was truly present with me. God spoke to me in that time of solitude, and maybe that's been your experience too. Have you found that, in those times when we feel we've exhausted all options, we can more clearly hear from God? When we are in the worst place ever imagined, God becomes incredibly real to us. And when I am silent before God, I can hear Him speak. Not audibly, but in my spirit, through His Word, and through Christian counsel. God really does speak to us when we're sitting in the ashes.

So let me offer some practical steps for inviting God to shine His light into your darkness. Are you familiar with the book of Job? Considered by God a righteous man, Job is described as blameless, upright, fearing (or respecting) God, and intentional about turning away from evil (Job 1:1, 8). Yet God allowed Job to experience much tragedy. In his experience of great loss and immeasurable pain, Job showed us how to sit in the ashes so God can shine on our brokenness His light of healing and hope. Here are a few lessons we can learn from Job:

1. **Arise**. After hearing the crushing news that his oxen, donkeys, sheep, camels, the servants tending them, and all of his sons and daughters had been killed, Job "arose, tore his robe, [and] shaved his head" (Job 1:20). Now—and thankfully—God is not calling us to tear our clothes or shave our head, but He is calling us to be intentional in seeking Him. And I believe that when Job arose from the ashes, he was taking his first step of seeking God in his darkness.

Like Job, we have an important choice to make when we receive heartbreaking news, and our decision will determine whether or not we will one day live in freedom. The question is "Whom will you seek?" If you choose yourself or your spouse, a friend or a pastor, you are giving the power to heal your heart to a limited and fallible soul. If you choose to seek God, however, you are allowing the One who is called Healer to mend your broken heart. Job's outward actions of tearing his robe and shaving his head are physical representations of his choice to seek God. Whom will you seek, my friend? Upon making your decision, arise.

2. **Surrender** and call out to God. He hears you, my beloved. So, speaking out loud, tell the Lord exactly what you're thinking and feeling. Yes, at times we speak with God through journaling or silent prayer, but amazing transformation occurs when I speak out loud whatever I'm experiencing inside. This act seems to both send Satan away and invite the Lord to be even more present with me. You may be afraid to say out loud what you're thinking and feeling, fearful that the pain will become even more real. Remember, the Lord knows what is on your heart even before you speak it. Know, too, that this process of calling out to God is for your benefit. It is an opportunity for you to be authentic with your Savior.

I've heard women say, "I have never questioned God" as if that's something to be proud of. Dear one, anytime we are in a genuine relationship with someone, we'll have questions. That's natural and normal. A healthy relationship between people who trust each other can handle questions, even hard questions, that are asked with humility, gentleness, respect, and love. God can handle your questions too. So take your hard questions to the Lord and ask Him. Perhaps you long to ask your Savior and Lord these questions:

- **Where were You, Lord, when** _____**?** You fill in the blank. Here are my questions: *Where were You, Lord, when I was being sexually abused all those years? Where were You, Lord, when the murderer faced my elderly parents? Where were You, Lord, when my baby Rachel's heart stopped beating?*
- **Lord, why did You allow** _____ **to happen to me?** Again, my dear, with authenticity and transparency, fill in the blank. And, again, here are my questions: *Why did You allow me, an innocent child, to be abused? Why did You allow my parents to be murdered? The murderer could have entered any house. Why my parents' house? Why 802 Washington Avenue in Albany, New York? And why—just a few short months after my parents were murdered and my heart was already so broken—why did you allow my baby to die? I wasn't able to heal from one tragedy, and You, Lord, allowed another to come. I don't understand, Lord. I thought You were good.*

As Job did, pour out your heart to God (Job 29-31). Your heavenly Father longs to hear from you. He won't be angry with you. He loves you, and He will always listen.

3. **Hear** from the Lord. Once you have chosen to arise, seek the Lord, and be genuinely transparent with Him, you will be able to receive from the Lord. Know, for instance, that the Lord desires to comfort you. When my parents were murdered, I desperately needed to hear from the Lord. I struggled with questions and, at times, overwhelming emotion. When I needed to have my time with the Lord, my husband

would take our ten-month-old to the park to play. I would then place myself in a position to hear anything the Lord spoke to me, and He did speak. The Lord spoke to Job (chapters 38—41) and to me, but He didn't answer our many questions the way we answer each other's questions. Instead, the Lord spoke to me in my spirit, through His Word, through Christian counsel, and through the stories of others who have confronted Him about the pain in their life.

4. **Engage** with the Lord. Don't just read the Word of God; engage and interact with it. Look up what Scripture says about ideas you're struggling with. Find answers to your questions in the Bible. Write on an index card the Scriptures that minister most to you and meditate on them. Dear one, whenever you think the Lord has spoken to you, write down what you think He said. Remember that His words will always align with Scripture; He will never say or ask you to do anything contrary to His Word. Even if a Christian sister, pastor, or friend says, "The Lord told me to tell you…" be sure that message is consistent with the Word of God. Regardless of our age, we will always need wise counsel—and we always need to be sure the counsel we receive is grounded in God's truth, in the Bible. Because God is the same yesterday, today, and forevermore (Hebrews 13:8), His truth—presented in His Word—will always be the same. Our unchanging God is reliable and trustworthy. He is our Rock.

When Job heard from the Lord, he responded to what the Almighty said (see Job 40—42). And as the Lord spoke to Job and Job spoke to the Lord, Job experienced God's presence in a powerful way. Job said, "I had only heard about you before, but now I have seen you with my own eyes" (42:5 NLT). Similarly, during those times of great suffering in my life, I began to really know God—and then I began to know Him better. I would experience in a very powerful way His presence with me. Also, the words in the Bible that describe His character are no longer black and white marks on a page; those words are life for me. The truth those words express has become alive and active in me, allowing me to experience God's love, worship His character, and find hope in His goodness.

James 5:11 reads, "We call blessed those who showed endurance. You have heard of the endurance of Job, and you have seen the purpose of the Lord, how the Lord is compassionate and merciful." Right now, in the midst of your suffocating pain, is *not* the time to give up on the Lord. Instead, remain, endure, and persevere. God wants to reveal Himself to you; He wants you to know Him better. I didn't know God's beautiful light until I was living in great darkness.

5. **Speak** forth God's goodness. Spend time acknowledging who God is. These names of God—just a few of many—may encourage you:

- *Elohim* – The Strong Creator God
- *El Roi* – The God Who Sees
- *Jehovah Shalom* – The God of Peace
- *Jehovah Rapha* – The God Who Heals
- *Jehovah Raah* – The Lord Is My Shepherd

Praise the Lord in words and song. Write in your journal about His goodness and love. Even on the difficult days when you don't feel it—as Nike says—"Just do it!" On good days, on not-so-good days, and on days when you don't even want to get out of bed, speak God's truth to your broken heart. Preach a sermon to yourself. Remember that Satan is a liar and the father of lies (John 8:44). Rebuke him— send him away—and replace his lies with God's truth.

Our purpose in life is to glorify God. We do this best as we walk closely with Him and seek to imitate Him. As He molds us more and more into His image, the better we represent Him to others. And we want to do that not only because God calls us to, but because Jesus is the Hero of our stories. Let me reassure you that, as you begin to heal, my friend, you will be able to point others to Jesus. You will be able to speak about how good God was in your darkness. Keeping at the forefront of your mind the ways God met you in the most difficult seasons of your life is essential to your healing and wholeness.

As I close this section, I encourage you to invite the Lord to shine His light into your darkness. Then, let the acronym ASHES remind you to *Arise, Surrender, Hear, Engage,* and *Speak*.

PERSONAL REFLECTION AND APPLICATION

1. It's time for you to apply to your life the truth you found in this chapter. What aspects of Emily's brokenness did you identify with? Why? What encouraged you about the ways the Lord shined His light into Emily's darkness? Be specific.
2. I hope that, by now, you are convinced of the need to come out of hiding (chapter 1) and to invite God to shine His light into your darkness (chapter 2). Take out a journal, perhaps one you can dedicate to the Lord as a record of His healing work in your life. Take some time—even a short ten minutes, but you may need or want more—to look again at the practical steps of sitting in the ashes: arise, surrender, hear, engage, and speak. How well are you doing? What encouragement do you find in these steps and in the possibilities of this process? What call to action? What do you see about yourself—and what will you do in response?

PRAYER: *Lord Jesus, I am in a place of intense darkness. I need Your help: please rescue me from this pit of despair and hopelessness. I choose to arise from the ashes and seek You. And, despite all my questions and doubts, I surrender to You. Open my ears to hear from You, Lord. With the help of the Holy Spirit who lives in me, enable me to engage with You, with Your Word, and with Your truth. Penetrate my darkness with Your light... and empower me to speak of Your goodness. As You continue to heal me, enabling me to live in freedom, allow me the privilege of shining Your light into other people's darkness. In the name of the One who sat with me in my darkness, in the name of Jesus Christ, I pray.*

CHAPTER **THREE**

A Context for Healing and Growth

BELOVED, I HOPE YOU'VE realized that you aren't alone in your intense pain and profound heartache. Like you and countless others, I, too, have known great suffering. Perhaps, you are in a season of brokenness right now. I hope you hear me when I remind you that God loves you and will not forsake you (Hebrews 13:5). You may be too raw to believe these truths for yourself. If that's the case, know that I'm believing for you. I'm grateful that God has led you to this book with its life-changing strategies that invite us to humbly receive healing from Jehovah Rapha, from "Our God Who Heals."

So, I hope you took the first biblical step of healing and came out of hiding. Maybe you've not only identified the source(s) of your pain, but you've also poured out your heart before the Lord and—not holding anything back—shared with Him about the ongoing impact of your devastating experiences on your day-to-day life. I trust that, as you brought your painful experiences into the light, God spoke to you, comforted you, and revealed more of Himself to you. I pray, my friend, that you will know God (Isaiah 43:10) and trust that He has good, redemptive, and hope-filled plans for you (Jeremiah 29:11).

Our suffering truly is the context for healing and growth—and I don't like that arrangement at all. I hate that suffering is when God changes me. I would prefer God speaking His truth to me and doing His best molding of my character in times of joy. Yet as a believer in Christ, I know that God will bring much good from our painful, difficult circumstances (Romans 8:28). He will mold you—and me—more into the image of His Son, Jesus. I know you will find healing and hope in your seasons of suffering just as my dear friend Vanessa did. After you read her story, I will point out how Vanessa followed the Bible's road map to freedom.

> *I was born to an alcoholic dad and a codependent mom. Dad grew up in a two-room house with his abusive, alcoholic father and his mother who would never consider divorce. Dad joined the Navy to get away from all of that and to see the world. His sailor buddies enjoyed buying women and alcohol when they were on shore leave, and Dad joined in. He met my mom through a buddy.*
>
> *Mom came from a family of German descent. I have limited memories of them, but I do remember my grandfather swearing a good bit. I know my mom loved her parents deeply—especially her grandfather Pappa. Neither of Mom's parents attended church, but Pappa would take her to church, sit in the car, and read the newspaper while she went in. And that's how Mom raised my sister and me. She always wanted us to have access to a church even though she and Dad did not attend. God was not talked about much and Christianity certainly was not practiced in our home.*
>
> *Dad would get drunk and angry, and there would be yelling and lots of profanity. Mom would rush my sister and me off to bed early when he'd had too much:*

"Hurry up and get into bed. Your dad's had too much to drink." The urgency and concern in her voice made it clear we should do as she said. A couple of times Dad got physical: he threw things and slammed doors. He got mad at my sister one time and pinned her up against the back of the couch while yelling at her. It looked to me like he was choking her.

My sister and I were afraid that Mom and Dad were going to divorce. We talked about it at night in the bed we still shared, and we decided between ourselves that one of us would go with each of them so neither of them would have to live alone. A few times Dad got mad and stormed out of the house. After a while, Mom would load up my sister and me in the pickup, and we would drive down to the local bar. We had to lock the doors and stay in the truck because we weren't old enough to go in. Mom would go in, and somehow Dad would wind up coming back home.

Having decided to come out of hiding (chapter 1), Vanessa identified the sources of her pain: alcoholic dad, codependent mom, and no foundation of Christian faith. As Vanessa named the sources of her pain, she acknowledged the destructive pattern that began generations earlier. Vanessa's abusive and alcoholic dad grew up with an abusive and alcoholic father. Her dad had a choice: would he live free of addiction, or would he follow in his dad's footsteps? Vanessa's father became an alcoholic and—as you will read below—Vanessa did too.

Another unhealthy pattern was that neither her parents nor her grandparents had a relationship with the Lord. Although Vanessa was exposed to "church," no adult modeled the life of a born-again believer.

VANESSA ASKED JESUS TO SHINE HIS LIGHT

Usually more than just one or two people cause us pain. Often, though, we can bring pain on ourselves. Vanessa continues her story:

> *Before I was thirteen, I had discovered boys and alcohol. I shudder now to think how young I was, but I had found that these two things made me feel either very good about myself or feel nothing at all—and I was always needing one or the other. So my days of self-medicating began.*
>
> *I met my first husband when I was 18 years old. He was in his thirties and married with two kids. I was drunk. He was probably drunk too. I didn't ask him to, but he left his wife and a couple years later he asked me to marry him. I didn't know what love was, and this seemed as close to love as anything I'd heard anybody describe, so I said yes. I always describe that relationship as having "met drunk, dated drunk, married drunk, and divorced drunk." The experience was hurtful and harmful, and I fought alcoholism for many years after that.*
>
> *After the divorce, I immediately met my next husband, who I am still married to today. He is significantly older than I am, and he was going through a tough breakup at the time. He had been raised in church but had fallen away from it. Both of us had been married, so both of us were afraid to make another commitment. We dated for five years before he asked me to marry him.*
>
> *We got married, and all was fine for a while. But I unexpectedly got pregnant and had a baby boy. I started taking our son to church before he could walk, and I guess some of it rubbed off on me. I was baptized when he was less than two years old. I was changing, but my husband wasn't—and the result was massive*

conflict in our marriage. Our relationship spiraled
downward. Further and further down it went. Conflict
after conflict. Sin after sin. I hit rock bottom. We wound
up in a crisis that required both of us to extend to the
other much forgiveness and grace.

As you'll see below, at this point in Vanessa's story, she took the second biblical step toward living in freedom. When Vanessa hit rock bottom, she asked God to shine His light into her darkness. She began taking this step when she invited the Lord into her heart and then was baptized, an act of obedience to Jesus that represented the inner rebirth that had occurred. Even after we recognize that Jesus has saved us from the eternal consequences of our sin, it takes us time and courage to truly surrender every aspect of our life and all of our heart to Him.

Vanessa's marriage continued to spiral downward, and she continued to go through the motions of life alone, daily walking in darkness, walking in sin. The deep and heart-wrenching molding of her character began when Vanessa called out to God. She raged at Him and asked the hard questions we all want answered. Like Job, whom we discussed in the previous chapter, Vanessa *arose* to seek God. She *surrendered* and called out to God. Vanessa *heard* from the Lord. She *engaged* with Him. And she *spoke* of God's goodness to many, including me. Hear more from Vanessa:

Thanks to God and some precious born-again believers
who He put in my life, I got out of that pit. It was a long
journey. But over the next year, I experienced some
major spiritual growth. My preacher's wife became my
best friend. She walked closely with me, helping me to
know God and to develop a real relationship with Him.

I still remember the first time I made the conscious
decision not to lie. I was taking a class and wanted to
go to a revival at our church on a night we had class.
My first instinct was to tell the teacher I didn't feel well

and just skip class. Instead, I told her I wanted to go to church revival. And it worked! The truth worked! That may sound silly to you, but it was a revelation that meant freedom to me. I could simply tell the truth!

Vanessa could tell the truth because Jesus *is* the truth. Satan is a liar, the father of all lies (John 8:44). Also, since Vanessa had surrendered to Jesus' lordship over her life, she was experiencing real change and healing.

SAVIOR VERSUS LORD

Many of us are familiar with the Bible verse John 3:16: "For God so loved the world that he gave his only Son, so that everyone who believes in him may not perish but may have eternal life." At first, Vanessa was like many of us who surrender to the Lord as our *Savior*, but our lives don't immediately change. It was many years after her baptism—when her second marriage began falling apart—that Vanessa surrendered to her Savior as *Lord*.

As Romans 10:9 states, "If you confess with your lips that Jesus is Lord"—that He is King over your life—"and if you believe in your heart that God raised Jesus from the dead"—that He, your Savior, defeated death and saved you from eternal death—"you will be saved." You may be saved, but are you experiencing real transformation in your life? If not, maybe you've accepted Jesus as your Savior, but not yet as your Lord. Naming Jesus as your Lord means surrendering every aspect of your life to Him; it means allowing Him to change you. By God's grace and in His power, you also need to live according to His ways.

And God's plan for living in freedom is what this book is about, and this book is based on the Bible, on God's Word. We need to know God's Word and let it shape our life. When we do, we will be living with Jesus as our Lord. Many people, however, will accept that Jesus died on the cross for their sins, but they stop there. They don't live with their Savior as their Lord, and they won't know true freedom.

You see, my friend, the life of freedom requires us to allow Jesus, our Savior, to reign over us—and over every aspect of our life—as our Lord. He calls us to live in a manner pleasing to Him and, by the power of His Holy Spirit, enables us to do so. Living with Jesus as our Lord and with the Bible as our road map will mean living in freedom.

AMBIVALENCE

Feeling ambivalent—having both positive and negative feelings about our life experiences and the people involved—is quite common during the healing process. As Vanessa engaged with the Lord, she realized that this tension between positive and negative feelings can often be quite confusing when we first shine God's light into that darkness. It's hard to accept that the people who have wounded us deeply are usually not completely evil. The Lord came alongside Vanessa and made her aware of, for instance, her father's kindness:

> *My dad was a good guy. I remember him tending to a down-the-road neighbor who lived in poverty and was usually drunk. One day the neighbor was limping badly as he made his way down the road. When Dad asked him what happened, Dad found out that he and his son had gotten into an argument, and the son had shot him in the foot. This neighbor didn't want to call the cops on his son. So Dad brought him up on our porch, got the alcohol and iodine, and fixed him up with ointment and bandages. After telling him how to clean the wound and change the dressing, Dad sent him on his way with some additional bandages.*

Vanessa also tells about a time that reveals her daddy's heart for her and her sister—the kind of story that many of us wish we could share about our own father:

I remember when some neighborhood teenage boys were picking on my sister and me as we were riding horses. We had almost finished our ride and were less than half a mile from home. The boys were slowly driving by us, revving the engine to try to spook our horses, and laughing at us.

At my sister's urging, I raced my horse home as fast as I could, yelling to Mom, "They're going to get Sally!" Mom screamed for Dad, and he came running up from the barn. After getting just enough information—through my tears and screams—to know that Sally was in trouble, he ran around to the front of the house just as the teenagers were driving by.

Without hesitating, Dad ran out in front of the car. I can still picture him standing spread-eagle in the middle of the road, so they had to stop the car. Then Dad went around to the front passenger-side window, reached in, grabbed the boy sitting there by the front of his shirt, pulled him halfway out of the car through the open window, and then yelled at him, nose to nose, "What did you do to my girls?!"

Word got around, and we never had any similar trouble after that.

Vanessa also shares some fond memories of her mom:

I remember Mom signing us up for band as early as elementary school and buying our instruments. She got us piano lessons too. And I remember when she signed us up for dance classes in the next town about 20 miles away. She would check us out of school early and drive us to those classes. I remember when they bought us a three-foot pool for the back yard, and Mom, Sally, and I installed it ourselves, shoveling the dirt and pressing it down until it was level. Those really were fun times.

⊰ TINA C. ELACQUA, PH.D. ⊱

Vanessa is able to acknowledge this puzzling truth: "My mom and dad really did try to love us, protect us, and do lots of things for us." Again, please know that you are perfectly normal if you have both positive and negative feelings toward those who have done you wrong. You may even have both positive and negative feelings toward the unwanted and unasked-for circumstances that brought profound pain, and this is normal too. For example, I am grateful for how much more I know the Lord now post-tragedy. However, I still don't appreciate the painful circumstances that provided me with an opportunity to know the Lord better. Don't rob yourself of healing by making the person or the circumstances all wrong. If, for instance, Vanessa could only see her parents' mistakes, she would not have been able to heal. The reason is, if you allow yourself to only focus on the wrongs done to you—on the darkness, the pain, and the turmoil those deeds have brought—you become bitter, and that bitterness may block the good work the Lord wants to do in you, through you, and in the midst of the circumstances (Hebrews 12:14-15; Romans 8:28). I've had to tell myself that truth again and again.

As I shared, I was molested for years. At first my only feelings toward him were hatred and anger. I could say nothing good about him. But after I invited Jesus into my life and began allowing Jesus to heal my pain, I started to understand forgiveness. As I embraced the forgiveness God has given me (I'll talk about this more in chapter 5), I was able to forgive this molester. In fact, I was able to see that he—like me—is a broken individual living in a fallen world. I was able to experience ambivalence (that's an improvement over hatred and anger!) and recognize both the bad things he did *to* me and the good things he did *for* me. Like many of the people who have deeply wounded us, this person was not all bad. And because I was now living with Christ as Lord of my life, I was able to acknowledge both the good and the bad.

Understanding this ambivalence is part of my story—part of everyone's stories—and it gave me some peace. So I encourage you, dear one, to embrace the ambivalent feelings you may have. Acknowledge them and give them to God.

EXPERIENCING GOD

Like Job—and like us—Vanessa didn't get answers to all the questions she asked the Almighty, but God did meet her in her suffering. He gave her His truth, He comforted her, and He healed her. In fact, when Vanessa was in her deepest, darkest pit, God met her there:

> *About a year after the marital crisis, I was asked to speak at a women's retreat. While preparing to speak, I prayed and fasted. I had been given a list of topics to choose from, and I had chosen to speak on being in the presence of God. He gave me an experience, I wrote about it, and it became part of my speech. Here it is:*
>
> *In that moment, I was in the presence of God. All my sins were laid bare. All the people in my life—past, present, and future—were there, and everyone could see everything I had ever done. Yet Jesus was seated at the right hand of God, declaring to His Father that I was innocent because He had died for me. So no one can accuse me. No one can "un-forgive" what God has forgiven.*
>
> *Then God stood up and started moving toward me. I was already on my knees, but I bent over at the waist into an upright fetal position. I recognized—I was overwhelmed by—His holiness, His purity, His greatness. I knew that when He reached me, I would be destroyed. I closed my eyes and curled up tightly, just waiting for the end.*
>
> *But I suddenly felt myself being lifted up from under my arms. God was lifting me up to His great height. And He held me close to His chest with my head tucked under His chin. Enfolding me in His embrace, He held me so tightly, and I realized how precious I was to Him. I felt His great love for me as He held me—His child—close. He just held me.*

Then I looked over His shoulder and saw Jesus. Still seated at the right hand of God's throne, He was beaming as He watched His Father's happiness. Jesus was pleased that His Father was holding one of His children. God turned, took me to Jesus, and gave me to Him. Together we watched as God picked up another one of His children—and Jesus just beamed. He had paid a high price, but this kind of love was why He had gone through all the agony. To see this, to watch the Father gather His children to Himself, one by one—I watched in awe and shared in His happiness.

STOPPING THE DESTRUCTIVE CYCLE

Like me, Vanessa lived in a dysfunctional family characterized by chaos, codependence, alcoholism, verbal and emotional abuse, and aggression. We both walked on eggshells and lived with uncertainty:

I grew up in an environment of mixed messages and mixed emotions. One minute, everything was good, but I was never sure what the next moment would bring. I always had to be on guard—half enjoying the moment I was in and half dreading the one that might come next. It was very confusing.

Even when I was a young child, I knew this was not the type of family I wanted for myself and any children I had (Lord willing) in the future. I decided that my family life would be different. I was committed to that goal, but I wasn't sure how to achieve it.

Well, I was fortunate enough to have a mother and father who, although not educated themselves, believed that their children would be. Even on a union worker's salary, my dad and my stay-at-home mom paid for my education. I believed that my getting an education would be one foundational way my family would look different from the one I grew up in.

Also, as I shared before, I was sexually abused, and I believe pornography fueled the perpetrator's evil acts. Unfortunately— although my perpetrator has not admitted it to me—I think he, too, was sexually abused. To whatever degree pornography contributed to the abuse I experienced, I was determined that pornography would have no place in my home, but forgiveness would. In fact, when I did get married, I asked this perpetrator to be in my wedding. What a loving God can do in the heart of His children is truly amazing.

When I was in high school, in college, and during various other seasons of my life, I sought counseling to find healing from the emotional damage caused by abuse. I knew that the shame, fear, and warped thinking needed to be exposed—brought into the light—if I were to bring closure to this part of my life. You see, women who are abused often choose a husband who abuses. I was determined not to let that happen, but I knew that the Lord needed to heal my mind so that I wouldn't fall into that trap.

Although my parents believed in Jesus, my family life did not model Christ's ways. Then, when I became a born-again believer in graduate school, I made the commitment to myself that I would not be unequally yoked: I would not marry someone who wasn't living with Jesus as his Savior and Lord. I was ready to wait however long for a husband who was also pursuing a life-giving, vital relationship with the Lord. I wasn't going to settle for an occasionally-go-to-church man. I would wait for a true follower of Christ, a man whose love for Jesus permeated every aspect of his being and every dimension of his life.

As you can see, I needed to think about my life and ask God to help me stop the destructive pattern that had robbed me of the abundant life Jesus came to give me. Over time, the Lord would make me aware of another pattern I would end.

When I was in Washington, DC, I was looking for a new job. I still remember the day I was at my friend's house using her computer and printer for the job application process. I was having a quiet time with the Lord, and He led me to Deuteronomy 30:15-20:

See, I have set before you today life and prosperity, death and adversity. If you obey the commandments of the LORD your God that I am commanding you today, by loving the LORD your God, walking in his ways, and observing his commandments, decrees, and ordinances, then you shall live and become numerous, and the LORD your God will bless you in the land that you are entering to possess.

But if your heart turns away and you do not hear, but are led astray to bow down to other gods and serve them, I declare to you today that you shall perish; you shall not live long in the land that you are crossing the Jordan to enter and possess.

I call heaven and earth to witness against you today that I have set before you life and death, blessings and curses. Choose life so that you and your descendants may live, loving the LORD your God, obeying him, and holding fast to him; for that means life to you and length of days, so that you may live in the land that the LORD swore to give to your ancestors, to Abraham, to Isaac, and to Jacob.

My dear friend, this Scripture provided me with such encouragement and the very real hope that my life could be different, better than anything I could have asked or imagined. Through this passage, God told me that my life could be radically different from what I had experienced growing up… and that by walking with the Lord and in His ways, by following His commandments, decrees, and ordinances, I would "live and become numerous" (hopefully that meant a husband and children). When I was invited to eight university campuses for job interviews, I asked the Lord each time, "Is this the position You will use to fulfill that Deuteronomy 30 passage in my life?"

Well, God led me to a small Christian college in Memphis, Tennessee. Saying yes to that job was another step on my path to healing. In August 1999, at my first faculty retreat, the Vice President of Academic Affairs led us in an opening devotional. He spoke about this same Scripture—Deuteronomy 30:15-20.

Approximately two years after this faculty retreat, at the age of 30, I met my husband. The abundant fruit of both character and deed that the Lord had produced in him, confirmed that he was the husband I had waited for. A year later we were married. In 2004, the Lord blessed us with our first girl. We lost our second baby girl in 2006. In 2007, the Lord gave us another baby girl.

As I reflect on my life, I see different times when I made an intentional decision to end a destructive pattern in my family, to end, for instance, the family line of alcoholism, pornography, sexual abuse, emotional/verbal/ physical abuse, lack of education, and the absence of a thriving relationship with Jesus. Don't think you have to decide immediately what pattern to tackle, but you will have to decide. I know you don't want to let Satan continue to destroy you and future family members, generation after generation. And I firmly believe that God will give you the courage and the wisdom today— and every day after that—to say, "The pattern ends with me! I will make sure that my children don't suffer the way I did. I will not allow alcoholism and drug addiction to continue. I will stop sexual abuse. I will remain faithful to my spouse. I will not get divorced."

At one point, for instance, Vanessa chose to stop the cycle of unforgiveness in her family:

> *I received unbelievable grace, forgiveness, and unconditional love from the Lord. Later in life I wound up writing an apology letter to my first husband's children. It was the right thing to do [in light of the fact that my affair with their dad had broken up their family].*

If the pain you experience is from poor choices you have made, today is a new day. God's mercies are new every morning. You can make a better choice—a Bible-based choice—that will help you experience God's freedom. Or perhaps the pain you experience today is simply the result of living in a fallen world. Still, you need to choose how to respond. I pray, beloved, that you will respond to life with joy in God, celebrating His grace to you, and singing praises for His mercy and love. Your choice to trust Jesus will be a powerful testimony of who He is as Shepherd, Healer, Redeemer, and Friend.

Dear one, will you embrace the One who provides healing and hope? Will you end the destructive pattern in your family for today, tomorrow, and future generations?

PERSONAL REFLECTION AND APPLICATION

1. Is Jesus both your Savior and your Lord? Explain. If Jesus isn't yet your Savior, please turn to "An Invitation to Know Christ" in chapter 1. If Jesus is not your Lord, ruling and reigning in your life, what aspects of your life are you holding back from Him? Why? Go before the Lord now and be completely transparent as you talk with the One who loves you enough to die for you.

2. What ambivalence do you feel toward the people who wounded you? What positive and negative thoughts and feelings do you feel toward the circumstances of those wounds? What destructive patterns in your life will you put a stop to? Be specific as you identify them. Start by saying, "No more!" Then ask the Lord to show you how to stop the pattern. Do you need professional counseling for help reframing your thoughts?

Many Christian counselors proved very beneficial to my healing, but sometimes just a simple step—like choosing not to drink—will be key to your healing. Since alcoholism runs in my family, my husband and I decided we wouldn't model drinking to our girls. We want to end the destructive pattern of alcoholism in our family. Spend time with the Lord and ask Him to show you the destructive patterns He wants you to end.

3. Dear one, I encourage you to embrace the first truth—that God allowed this evil to be done to you—as well as the second truth—that no wound has ever or will ever be inflicted on you that God cannot heal. Nothing is impossible with the Lord. He can heal your deepest wounds. He desires to restore you. So I implore you, friend, to choose to not live as a victim, but instead to trust that God will use your pain to mold you and make you more like Jesus.

What circumstances and experiences did God choose to use to mold you into His image? Was it a dysfunctional family, an alcoholic parent, an abusive husband, a special-needs child, an unjust boss, the loss of a loved one, or something else? Please reflect on the context (there may—and most likely will be—more than one) of God's healing and transformative work in your heart and life. Then meditate on this verse:

> *Though You have made me see troubles,*
> *many and bitter,*
> *you will restore my life again;*
> *from the depths of the earth*
> *you will again bring me up.* — Psalm 71:20 (NIV)

PRAYER: *Lord Jesus, thank You for being my Healer. I acknowledge that while I don't like the context(s) You used to shape me and mold me to look like Jesus, I am grateful that You don't abandon me in my pain. I am grateful that You give that pain meaning and purpose. As You sit with me in the ashes, You reveal Your presence with me. You bring me comfort, peace, and truth. You empower me to make better choices not only so I might know abundant life in You here on earth, but also for the benefit of future generations. You meet me in my pit of darkness and despair. You, Lord, tell me that You can lift me out of the pit of despair, destruction, and death. You lift me out of the mud and the mire; You set my feet on solid ground (Psalm 40:2). Come, Lord Jesus, take my hand and pull me out of this pit. Set my feet on solid ground and steady my legs so that I may go forth and tell of Your goodness.*

PART
TWO

Strategies for Living in Freedom

CHAPTER **FOUR**

Biblical Faith and Spiritual Disciplines

MY FRIEND LINDA SHARES her story here...

When I was twelve years old, my dad left. Sadly, my mom just fell apart and wasn't really able to be a parent. Since my older sister went with my dad, the responsibility of parenting my younger brothers fell to me. It was my job to make sure they were fed, got to school, etc. I didn't have a "normal" junior high/ high school experience at all. It seemed like no one in my family cared that I was missing out on being a kid. In their minds, the boys were the priority, and it didn't really matter what I was feeling. Actually, it's still this way.

My parents' lack of concern for me had a profoundly negative effect on me. I started to believe I didn't matter. Because no one cared that I was sad or upset, I came to the conclusion that my feelings didn't matter. I had suicidal thoughts. I began to self-harm. I let boys use me because I didn't see any worth in myself. I started skipping school. I was lucky to graduate high school at all because I'd missed so much.

In addition to all of this, my dad chose to fight for joint custody of only my brothers. He already had my sister. The fact that he didn't choose to fight for me cut me deeply. What did this say about me? Of four kids, I was the only one no one fought for. I know now that my dad was deeply hurt by my decision to stay with my mother (my sister and I were both old enough to choose who we wanted to live with full-time), but I still feel like he should have at least reached out to me and explained.

Anyway, all of this led me to one hard-and-fast conclusion: I was worthless and unlovable.

Well, as it usually does, all these childhood hurts came to a head: when I was nineteen years old, I got pregnant. The father of my child wasn't in the picture, and I felt this desperate need to escape what was happening in my life. To me, this baby represented staying in this dark place, and all I wanted to do was find some freedom. I chose to have an abortion. I didn't tell anyone. I just called a clinic, had a friend drive me, and was in, out, and back at home that same day.

After I did that, my life became even darker. I didn't realize it at the time, but my decision to have an abortion further cemented in my mind and heart that I was unlovable. I mean, I was a murderer. Who could love a murderer? I entered into abusive relationship after abusive relationship. I didn't take care of my body and ballooned to over 300 pounds. Throughout all of this, God wasn't a part of my life. To me, if my own family couldn't love me, how could God love me? Also, how could God even want to love me after the choices I'd made?

But then...God stepped in and changed my life. I began calling on the Lord when I was twenty-five. I just woke up one morning, and I wanted to go to church.

At church, on the large jumbo screen, there was an ad for a Christ-Centered Abortion Recovery. After looking at this ad for twenty minutes, I called the number. That was the moment God really stepped in and began to change me from the inside out. During subsequent meetings with the counselors, I heard an invitation to surrender my life to Jesus. I accepted wholeheartedly even though I was unsure of exactly what that meant.

Through my relationship with Jesus—through reading and studying God's Word, praying to my Lord, and worshipping Him when I'm by myself and at church—I was freed from my dark place of shame and depression. God showed me that He had the power to heal all of my wounds and that He wanted more for me than what I was giving myself. I have found such comfort in Him even when the world didn't have comfort to give me.

Now, just a few years later, I'm still on my special walk with Him. He's brought amazing people into my life who have continued to help me heal. He's led me down a path that I never would have imagined for myself. And I can honestly say—and I believe with all my heart—that God is my Father and He loves me. Granted, He still has to hit me over the head sometimes, especially when I start sliding back into my old thought processes, but I know He's there to pick me up. So I daily surrender to His will, not mine. And I choose to be in relationship with Jesus by talking or praying to Him about everything (Philippians 4:6) and reading His Word.

As Linda shared, being abandoned, feeling unloved and unlovable, contemplating suicide, choosing to have an abortion, carrying the guilt, struggling with obesity—a life characterized by these experiences as well as by physical, emotional, and sexual abuse is a life of darkness. And instead of being easy, bringing these painful experiences into the light requires great courage, as do the subsequent steps toward living in freedom from our past. Understanding the demands of healing, Jesus offered to this child of God—and He offers to you and me—the gifts of faith, the written Word, prayer, and worship, gifts that are necessary for walking in freedom.

Also helpful as we journey toward wholeness is learning from people who have gone before us. That's why I share other people's stories here: we can learn what helped them work through their pain and hear their practical advice for women who are hurting. This advice falls into two categories: internal strategies (chapters 4 and 5) and external strategies (chapters 6 and 7), both of which are essential for living in freedom from a painful past. Women who did not rely solely on other people to survive and thrive in the aftermath of their traumatic experiences adopted internal strategies that involved faith, God's Word, prayer, worship (chapter 4), and forgiveness (chapter 5), all of which are key to moving into a life of freedom. Women who applied external strategies to approach a life of freedom involved being a committed member of a vibrant church with biblical based resources and support for those who are struggling (chapter 6) and actively involved in a Christian community and professional counseling (chapter 7). Finally, chapter 8 will help you craft your own story based on all that you have learned in the first seven chapters and encourage you to share it as part of your healing process and for God's glory. In this chapter and the next, I will offer a biblical perspective on what the internal strategies I just mentioned entail as well as practical methods to help you use the strategies effectively on your own journey toward healing and freedom.

Biblical Faith

Foundational to living in freedom from our painful past is our faith, and the Holman Bible Dictionary definition of *faith* is helpful:

> Throughout the Scriptures faith is the trustful human response to God's self-revelation via His words and His actions. God initiates the relationship between Himself and human beings. He expects people to trust Him through what He says and does for the benefit of people who need Him. He provides evidence of His trustworthiness by acting and speaking in the external world to make Himself knowable to people who need Him. Thus, biblical faith is a kind of limited personal knowledge of God. (547)

To be specific, faith is believing that God will keep His promises to always love us, guide us, correct us, forgive us, provide for us, protect us, and be near us. Simply put, faith is believing God will do what He promised in Scripture He will do—and trusting in His faithful promise-keeping even when what is going on in our lives seems contrary to a fulfilled promise. We must choose faith particularly when we don't understand what God is up to, when we don't clearly see Him at work on our behalf, or when we don't feel His presence. After all, as we are reminded in Hebrews, "faith is the assurance of things hoped for, the conviction of things not seen" (11:1).

So... do you have faith? Do you have a personal relationship with the Lord Jesus that enables you to trust Him—to believe that He is who He says He is and that He will do what He says He will do? The first step to living free of the devastation of the past truly is a relationship with the Lord Almighty (see the Invitation to Know Christ in the sidebar of chapter 1).

Spiritual Disciplines: God's Word, Prayer, and Worship

When we place our faith in Jesus as our Savior and Lord, we receive—among many blessings—the gift of eternal life (John 17:2), the gift of assurance that we will forever be in God's presence. When we place our faith in Jesus, we also receive God's Holy Spirit who serves as our Advocate, Helper, Comforter, and Counselor, guiding and directing our steps as He keeps us mindful of what Jesus teaches in His holy Word (John 14:25-26). The Holy Spirit also equips us to live the abundant life Jesus came to give us (John 10:10). This same Spirit raised Jesus from the dead, and now He lives in us (Romans 8:11), working in our hearts to conform us to the image of Jesus Christ (Romans 8:29). May you—who are a believer in Christ—allow the Spirit who lives in you to use life's painful experiences for your good (Romans 8:28). Allow the Spirit to use the consequences of those experiences to mold you into the image of Jesus Christ (Romans 8:29), to transform your life so you will reflect Jesus Christ to others, and to enable you to minister to others with the comfort you have received from God (2 Corinthians 1:4).

You see, God's ultimate desire is for you and me to be like Jesus Christ (1 John 3:2-3). This is a process that will not be complete until we meet Jesus face-to-face (Philippians 1:6). Yet while we are on earth, we can use tools the Lord has provided to survive pain that has its roots in the past, to thrive in the aftermath of those hurts, and to become more like Jesus as, with every step we take, we draw closer to Him. And we draw closer to the Lord by participating daily in what are called spiritual disciplines. Don't let that phrase scare you away. These disciplines are tools the Lord gives us to know Him better and love Him more: He gives us His written Word, prayer, and worship.

THE FOUNDATION: GOD'S WORD

Many women I've counseled have told me their greatest challenge is finding daily time with God: they don't know how to integrate time with the Lord into the demands of their days. Of course extended time with the Lord—a weekend retreat, a day of silence at an abbey, even an hour alone in the park—is even harder to fit into the schedule. We all have the same twenty-four hours in a day. How is it that some women find time for the Lord, but others can't? After all, we do tend to make time for those things we most desire, right?

Jesus tells us to seek His kingdom first and He'll provide the other important things in time (Matthew 6:33). If we are truly seeking the Lord and His kingdom, then we will daily surrender to Him our minutes and hours. We will trust Him to guide us to live out kingdom priorities in the activities He has chosen for the day: He will ensure we spend time with Him. You see, when we align our life with the Lord's will and guidelines, He provides the time for us to complete all the important tasks He has given us to do. Of course we have our part to do too. Our part involves choosing to spend time with Him—taking that step of faith—even when a deadline looms, the playdate starts in five minutes, or you really need to make those phone calls to line up volunteers for vacation Bible school.

Now, before you start beating yourself up or feeling burdened with guilt, know that our time with God will look different in different seasons of life. Also remember He's the One who gave you the kids, work, elderly parents, church role, etc. that contribute to your feeling you don't have time to open the Bible. Find peace in the truth that your gracious heavenly Father knows your heart.

Let me remind us (yes, I'm reminding myself, too) of the value of spending time with God. Maybe you've felt like Katie has: "I've had times when I questioned God. Not whether He was real, but just what significance He had in my everyday life." God has great significance because He *is* our life: He gives us purpose for our days and a place in His family. Furthermore, Jesus describes Himself as our Shepherd (John 10:11, 14), and we are the sheep in His flock (Psalm 95:7). Like typical sheep, we aren't very smart, and we tend to go our own way. But the Lord, our good Shepherd, desires to draw us near to Him (Isaiah 40:11), and He goes after us when we stray (Matthew 18:12-14; Luke 15:3-7). When we yield to the care of our Shepherd, we receive His tender love, His comfort, and His guidance for everyday living.

The Bible, however, does more than offer solid guidelines for how to live. In Hebrews 4:12, we learn that "the word of God is living and active, sharper than any two-edged sword, piercing until it divides soul from spirit, joints from marrow; it is able to judge the thoughts and intentions of the heart." In 2 Timothy 3:16, we read, "All scripture is inspired by God and is useful for teaching, for reproof, for correction, and for training in righteousness." In order for God to use His Word to conform us to the image of Jesus, we must make time to read the Bible.

When we do, we will find that God's Word is alive and powerful: it helps us recognize our sin; it helps us understand the plan He has for us straying, sinful human beings He created; and it helps us know Jesus, our Savior and Lord. In the New Testament, Jesus' teachings and the letters written to the early church offer practical guidelines for living as God's light in this world, as His ambassadors of truth, and as disciple-makers in our family and around the globe. God's Spirit uses the written Word to guide us, to enable us to recognize God's voice, and to make us more like Jesus in character and heart.

Despite the richness and power of the Bible, a 2013 *Bible Archaeology* article reports that "one of the most serious problems facing the Church in the 21st century is the problem of Biblical illiteracy. Simply put, most professing Christians do not possess a sound and coherent understanding of the Bible, beginning with sound doctrine and general Biblical history." If Christians don't know God's Word and therefore don't live by it, our lives will look and be a lot like the lives of non-Christians. We will make the same poor choices; we will walk down the same road to destruction.

A Practical Tool: Making Time to Be with the Lord and Read His Word

Let me offer you six practical tips to help you spend time with the Lord:

- Remind yourself of the value and the blessing of spending time with Jesus.

- Give yourself grace when you miss a day, or two, or three. Remember, God loves you and desires to spend time with you. If you find yourself low on desire—if spending time with God seems more of a "have to" than a "get to"—God already knows that. So ask Him to change your heart, to give you a genuine desire to spend time with Him. After all, He loves you, and He is the One who will heal you as you get to know Him better, as you learn more about His character, His ways, His thoughts, and His heart for you. Don't be legalistic about checking off a "Spend time with the Lord" box. Rather, ask God to work in your heart so that you come to look forward to the opportunity and the privilege you have to spend time with your Creator, your Lord, your King, your heavenly Father, your Shepherd.
- Determine the best time of the day for you to sit quietly with the Lord and His Word—and keep that appointment daily. Protect that time and don't let interruptions rob you of those sacred minutes.
- Choose a Bible reading plan. Many structured formats for reading your Bible are available. You could, for instance, read the book of Matthew, one of four accounts of Jesus' life. You might choose a study that has an Old Testament passage, a New Testament passage, and a psalm for every day. Perhaps you will purchase a Bible study guide with questions that facilitate a better understanding of a specific book. You have many choices. Find one that works well for you.
- When you sit down with Jesus, set a timer so you don't keep interrupting yourself to check the time.
- Join a Bible study or Sunday school class where you dig deeper into God's Word—and where people wonder where you are if you don't show up!

Many Bible study resources are available. I am slightly biased in favor of the free resources offered through Doral Cove Ministries. These articles and radio segments will teach you how to live every day for Christ. All the material is anchored in God's Word, and all explain how to apply His Word to the ups and downs of everyday life. It is only when we know and obey God's Word that we live the abundant life He has for us.

PRAYER

Simply put, prayer is having a conversation with the Lord. Imagine Jesus sitting across the table from you or on the couch next to you. Talk to Him as you would a friend. He longs to be your best friend— and unlike our earthly friends, He is available 24/7.

In His Word, the Lord promises to answer us when we cry out to Him in prayer (Jeremiah 33:3), and He will answer every prayer with "Yes," "No," or "Wait." God always hears our requests, and He always responds in accordance with His will—His good and perfect will.

In 1 Thessalonians 5:16-18 God calls us to pray continually: "Rejoice always, pray without ceasing, give thanks in all circumstances; for this is the will of God in Christ Jesus for you." As we walk through our day, we keep open the lines of communication with the Lord Almighty, being mindful of Him moment by moment.

When we pray, we open ourselves to the Lord's good work of renewing our minds. The Lord tells us in Romans 12:2, "Do not be conformed to this world, but be transformed by the renewing of your minds, so that you may discern what is the will of God—what is good and acceptable and perfect." A renewed mind is a Christ-centered mind and a mind focused on the specific truth from God's Word that pertains to the aspects of life where we are struggling. Inspired and impacted by God's character, guided by His Word, and regenerated by the work of the Holy Spirit, a renewed mind is a mind that thinks and sees with an eternal-kingdom perspective.

A renewed mind is also a mind focused on who God is and on His unchanging, life-giving truth. As Philippians 4:8 reads, "Whatever is true, whatever is honorable, whatever is just, whatever is pure, whatever is pleasing, whatever is commendable, if there is any excellence and if there is anything worthy of praise, think about these things." We ask God to help us to "destroy arguments and every proud obstacle raised up against the knowledge of God, and we take every thought captive to obey Christ" (2 Corinthians 10:4-5).

And that's where praying Scripture comes into play. Incorporating phrases and even entire verses from Scripture in our prayers is a way of grounding ourselves in God's Word and being focused on God's truth and on who He is. With that grounding and that focus, we are cooperating with God: He wants to renew our minds—to help us think the way He thinks and to protect our mind from the enemy's lies—for His glory and our good.

Also, I've found that speaking out loud to God when I pray keeps me more focused on the conversation and more aware of His presence with me. Sometimes, especially when life is overwhelming, I choose to write out my specific prayers to God based on the truths and promises found in His Word.

A Practical Tool: Praying Scripture to Reinforce Faith and Develop a Renewed Mind

I was like many of the women I have counseled: what has most helped me endure incredibly painful trials and eventually thrive in the aftermath is my belief in God. Regardless of how much my heart was—and sometimes still is—troubled, I choose to believe in God, and I pray words from Scripture to reinforce my faith.

When I lost my parents and, soon after that, my baby Rachel, I needed God's Word more than I ever had before. I also needed help processing and managing the many intense feelings and potentially crippling behaviors that had arisen (see below). And I knew where to turn. As God enabled me to write *Hope Beyond Loss: A Biblical Framework for Surviving and Processing Loss* and then to teach it year after year, I saw that group members displayed certain feelings and behaviors. So, regardless of the kind of trauma and pain they had experienced in life, they were able to identify with one another's feelings as well as with behaviors indicative of past trauma. As you review the following list of feelings and behaviors, note which ones you've dealt with:

Feelings and Behaviors Resulting from Life Experiences

- Aloneness (isolation; no support group)
- Anger, bitterness, rage
- Anxiety and worry
- Being stuck in my grief and current circumstances
- Depression (beyond just sadness or the blues)
- Fear
- Financial challenges
- Guilt and sense of condemnation
- Inability to understand what happened, how to go on living, what to do next
- Lack of focus; feeling distracted
- Physical ailments (headaches, fatigue, exhaustion, panic attacks)
- Sense of inadequacy
- Sleep problems (too much, too little, nightmares)
- Unwanted and intrusive thoughts

This list is not exhaustive. Feel free to add to it and to make it personal: What other unhelpful feelings and behaviors have resulted from your life experiences?

Next, take a look at the chart "Persistent Feelings and Behaviors: God Can Bring Freedom" (page 60). Using the list and/or the chart, choose an aspect of your life or your heart for which you would like to receive healing. Don't worry if you find more than one issue you'd like to work on. All of us have more than one! The good news is, we don't need to tackle everything at once. Choose just one for right now, maybe the one that is most pressing at the moment. I'll share an example from my own life:

I wasn't present when my parents were murdered, and I was haunted by thoughts of what had happened. Daily, I was plagued with these unwanted and intrusive ideas. I felt tormented by the images and thoughts of my parents' departure from earth. The more I agonized over my parents' painful deaths, the more I reviewed the scene over and over again in my mind, and the more tortured I felt. The more I focused on the ugliness, the more deeply I was drawn into despair. To stop that movement, I asked God for a renewed mind and began praying relevant Scripture. Every time my mind wandered or imaginings of my parents' last moments on earth entered my mind, I replaced those destructive thoughts with the Scriptures I had chosen to pray. I wanted Him to renew my mind by freeing me from such thoughts.

You see, friends, when we pray God's Word over our circumstances—over our loss, our fear, or our pain—we invite God to help us to see this earthly life from His perspective, and we welcome His use of Scripture to mold us more into the glorious likeness of Jesus. After all, it is God's Word that the Holy Spirit uses to comfort us, give us hope in the darkness, renew our minds, and transform us into the image of Christ. May we cooperate with God's Spirit as He renews and protects our minds.

Persistent Feelings and Behaviors: God Can Bring Freedom

Justice	Dealing with Extended and Immediate Family, Friends, Media, Justice System, Workplace, Crime Scene, Investigation, Trials, Sentencing, Medical Examiner or Coroner, Funeral/Memorial Service, Plea-Bargains, The Unsolved Case, A Not-Guilty Verdict
Life After a Loss	Making Peace with the Past, Spiritual Growth/Positive Outcomes, Forgiveness and Renewal, Rediscovery of the Meaning of Life, Making Meaning of the Tragedy, Good Memories, Surviving, Finding Joy Again, Dealing with Holidays/Birthdays/Special Occasions, Coping/Managing Strategies, Feeling Safe Again, Helping Others
Physical Symptoms	Headaches, Depression, Anxiety, Panic Attacks, Paralyzed by Pain, Jumpiness, Constant Crying, Addictions, Extended Grief That Interferes with Life
Feelings & Symptoms	Grief, Shock, Confusion, Fear, Anger, Revenge, Frustration, Survivor Guilt, Regret, Lack of Control/Power, Numbness, Self-Blame, Lack of Focus
Saying Goodbye	Loss of Dreams, Hopes, and a Future with the Deceased, Sadness, Never Forgetting the Loved One, Changed Priorities
Sleep Problems	Sleepless Nights, Too Much Sleep, Nightmares
Spiritual Life Issues	The Sovereignty of God, The Presence of God, Hope vs. Despair, Crushed in Spirit, Need for Comfort, Sense of Aloneness, Anger at God, Disappointment with God, Unanswered Questions (e.g., Why, Lord? What if…?), God as Restorer, A Deeper Appreciation of Life, Greater Intimacy with the Lord, Healing
Support Network	Emotional and Social Support Groups/Networks, Professional Help/Counseling, Surviving, Calls/Cards Stop Coming, Friends/Family Members Avoid You, People Say Stupid Things or Nothing at All, Re-Traumatization
Unwanted and Intrusive Thoughts	Flashbacks, Thoughts of Harming Yourself or Others, Triggers
Vigilance	Worry About the Safety of Loved Ones and Your Own Personal Safety, Avoidance of People or Places

Your Turn: Praying Scripture

The process of praying Scripture is simple. Consider for what present situation you need and want God's comfort, direction, and hope. Be specific about both the circumstances and your feelings. Then look up what God's Word has to say about those feelings and incorporate what God says into your prayer.

Choose, for instance, a feeling or behavior and complete the first part of this sentence:

I feel _____, but God's Word tells me_____.

OR

Lord, I need healing and freedom from _____.

I ask You to renew my mind.

Did you notice that completing both sentences requires us to be truthful, honest, and authentic in our inward beings (Psalm 51:6)? To reach that point, you might find it helpful to write about or draw a picture that reflects what you are thinking and feeling about the matter for which you desire freedom from pain and a renewed mind. Don't stifle any thoughts and feelings. Don't critique or edit yourself. Let your memories, ideas, thoughts, and feelings pour out of you so the Lord can contain them and heal you.

Having identified our feelings and/or a specific request for healing, we are ready to open God's Word. Maybe you're not familiar with what the Bible says about that feeling or behavior you identified, and that's OK. The "God's Word for Life's Challenges" section at the back of this book lists some Scriptures for a variety of feelings and behaviors. That list may help you find Scripture that speaks to your situation. Here are some examples:

- I feel alone, but God's Word tells me He will never forsake me (Deuteronomy 31:6, 8; Joshua 1:5; Hebrews 13:5).
- I feel exhausted, but God's Word tells me to exchange my heavy burden for His light yoke (Matthew 11:28-30).

- I feel afraid, but God's Word tells me He did not give me "a spirit of fear and timidity, but of power, love, and self-discipline" (2 Timothy 1:7).
- I feel inadequate, but God's Word tells me that He can do all things, that nothing is impossible for Him, and that "I can do all things through him who strengthens me" (Mark 9:23; Ephesians 3:20; Philippians 4:13).
- I feel confused. I don't understand why God would take my loved one, but His Word tells me that His ways are not our ways and that He is the God of all comfort (Isaiah 55:8-9; 2 Corinthians 1:3-4).
- I feel condemned for my past sins, but God's Word tells me there is no condemnation for those who name Jesus as their Savior and Lord (Romans 8:1).

I encourage you to memorize the verse you incorporated into the *I feel* _____, *but God's Word tells me* _____ sentence above. Memorizing God's Word is one way we partner with God as He uses His truth to renew our mind and mold us into the image of His Son, Jesus. Scripture that helps you see your post-trauma feelings and behaviors from a biblical perspective may be good verses to start with as you make memorizing God's Word a priority.

As for the second sentence above, here's how I filled in the blank: *Lord, I ask for healing and freedom from unwanted and intrusive thoughts about my parents' last few moments on earth. I ask You to renew my mind.* You can use either this sentence or the *I feel...* sentence as a starting point for writing a brief prayer that incorporates the truths you have read in God's Word. Replace each lie, misperception, or inaccurate thought with God's truth. Address your troubling feelings with statements of divine comfort and assurance from Scripture.

Let me offer this example:

> *Lord, I ask for freedom from unwanted and intrusive thoughts regarding my parents' last few moments on earth. I desire a renewed mind. Please, Lord, replace*

the dark thoughts and the pain with the joys of the present.

Lord, I am encouraged when I choose to believe Your Word that my parents' moments of suffering do not compare to the glory my parents now enjoy. Paul wrote, "I consider that the sufferings of this present time are not worth comparing with the glory about to be revealed to us" (Romans 8:18). My mom and dad believed in You, Lord Jesus (Romans 10:9); therefore, when they became absent from the body, they were present with You (2 Corinthians 5:8). If given a choice, I know my parents would have chosen to be away from their bodies and at home with You (2 Corinthians 5:8; Philippians 1:23). I praise You, Lord, that in heaven there is no more fear or pain for my parents, but rather fullness of joy (Psalm 16:11).

Lord, I choose to discipline my mind to focus on the joy my parents now experience in the presence of Christ. Focusing on that truth brings me great peace and hope (1 Thessalonians 4:13-18). Thank You, Lord, for replacing my darkness of despair with thoughts of heavenly glory. Please continue to comfort my broken heart, Lord, with these truths. Amen.

One more thing. I find it very helpful—very powerful—to pray in front of a cross with my hands open, palms up. (If you don't have a cross in your home, the cross can be as simple as two twigs taped together.) With your hands in that position, you are saying to the Lord and demonstrating for yourself that you are releasing and surrendering to Him the thoughts that have been weighing you down. Simply put, you are inviting God to renew your mind. You are taking "every thought captive" in order to make it obedient to Christ (2 Corinthians 10:5), an act of obedience that will mean renewal. And in the process you have been feasting on and perhaps even memorizing God's life-giving Word.

So, precious one, every time your heart wanders and every time you find yourself face-to-face with your woundedness and pain, take out your prayer and pray it out loud to your all-powerful, all-loving God. When you do, you'll be blessed by God's healing presence and renewing grace.

WORSHIP

In addition to God's Word and the privilege of prayer He has granted us, God uses individual and corporate worship to help us live in freedom despite life's struggles.

What exactly is worship? The Holman Illustrated Bible Dictionary tells us that *worship* is "the act or action associated with attributing honor, reverence, or worth to that which is considered divine by religious adherents" (1686). As Christians, when we worship the almighty God of the Old Testament and the New, we are acknowledging the worth and honor that He is due.

A Practical Tool: Worship in the Day-to-Day

Romans 12:1 describes well the worship with our whole being that God desires: "Give your bodies to God because of all he has done for you. Let them be a living and holy sacrifice—the kind he will find acceptable. This is truly the way to worship him" (NLT). We are called to honor God in all we do, whether we are eating or drinking (1 Corinthians 10:31), speaking or doing (Colossians 3:17). We are also called to worship God with words of joyful praise and thanksgiving, such as young Mary did when she found out she would be the mother of Jesus (Luke 1:46-55). In everything we do, we—God's representatives on earth—are called to give Him glory by proclaiming His merit, value, and worth.

A tangible way that I worship the Lord is by remembering all He has done for me and the ways He has loved me. I find myself quick to forget God's faithfulness, so I set aside time to write down the specific ways God has worked in my life. I list answered prayers, surprises from God, ways He has intervened in my life, and times when He has done beyond what I could ever have asked and imagined. When I start to doubt God, His presence in my life, or His goodness, I take out my list of thanksgiving. That list quickly reminds me of this loving Lord who has never forsaken me and never will, and my heart overflows with worship and praise.

A Practical Tool: Worship Through Music

Psalm 150:3—5 describes what we often think of when we think of worship:

> Praise him with a blast of the ram's horn;
> praise him with the lyre and harp!
> Praise him with the tambourine and dancing;
> praise him with strings and flutes!
> Praise him with a clash of cymbals;
> praise him with loud clanging cymbals.

Playing musical instruments is certainly one method of worship, but our gracious God encourages those of us who are not musically inclined to "make a joyful noise" (Psalm 100:1). Hebrews 13:15 says, "Through Jesus, therefore, let us continually offer to God a sacrifice of praise—the fruit of lips that openly profess his name" (NIV). Giving my praise to the Lord through song glorifies Him and lifts my spirit. And He doesn't care if I sing off-key.

I remember many Sunday worship times when—with tears streaming down my face and my heart aching at the loss of my parents and baby Rachel—I would sing God's truth. Despite my feelings, I would revere the One who is holy. From that dark place, I chose to call out to the One who heals me. My worship truly was a "sacrifice of praise" that God honored: I could physically feel the darkness move away as I chose to praise my God (Hebrews 13:15).

Dear one, whenever you're down—whenever you're having the worst day ever or you're wondering if the darkness will ever pass—turn on music that inspires you, comforts you, and speaks to your soul. You will be fighting back the enemy who wants you to spiral down into deep despair. Relying on song, call on the One who will pick you up out of that miry pit and place you on a firm foundation (Psalm 40:2).

PERSONAL REFLECTION AND APPLICATION

This chapter has presented some concrete tools to help you live in freedom from the pain caused by life's struggles and hurts:

- Do you spend daily time with the Lord? What time of the day will you set aside for spending time with Him? Maybe you're a morning person; maybe you're a night owl. Find the time—day or night—that is best for you to spend time with Jesus and commit to reading and meditating on His Word at that time each day.
- What was the last Bible study or Sunday school class you participated in? Find a Bible-believing church that teaches the Word of God and sign up for a Bible study or Sunday school class.
- As you read this chapter, did you find one or two or even a handful of especially significant Scripture that the Lord used to speak truth to you? If so, choose to memorize one of those verses—and I know you could even get through that handful you listed. Memorizing verses and passages from God's Word is definitely worth the time and energy.
- What did you feel when, earlier in this chapter, you chose and wrote or maybe even drew about the matter for which you desire to have a renewed mind?
- Why might writing or drawing and applying God's Word to this matter help you heal?

- Share the prayer you wrote out with a friend or family member you trust who may be struggling with the same issues. Your prayer may provide them with encouragement as you point them back to Jesus.

May the truths in this chapter encourage you to spend time with the Lord, learning His truth, getting to know Him better, and living with the awareness that He is always with you, whatever your circumstances.

PRAYER: *Lord God, thank You that You empower me with faith. Faith that believes You are who You say You are. Faith that believes You will do what You say You will do. Thank You for Your precious Word that You use to transform me and make me more like Jesus. Thank You, too, in advance: I believe You will heal me and enable me to know freedom from this deep pain. Please renew my mind, so that I think Your thoughts, live according to Your priorities for me, know freedom from past pain, and accurately represent You to others as I shine forth Your love.*

References

Charles W. Draper, Chad Brand, Archie England, eds., *Holman Illustrated Bible Dictionary* (Nashville, TN: Holman Bible Publishers, 2003), 547.

Henry B. Smith, Jr., "Biblical Illiteracy" at Associates for Biblical Research, September 9, 2008, accessed April 4, 2018, http://www.Biblearchaeology.org/post/2008/09/Biblical-Illiteracy.aspx#Article.

CHAPTER **FIVE**

Forgiveness

LARA SHARES HER STORY below. I think it's one that all of us can relate to....

"You need to forgive God."

I was startled to hear those words. They sounded... if not heretical, at least irreverent. But lightning didn't strike.

You need to forgive God. *In an instant those words went from unsettling to piercing. My precious friend— my wise and godly friend Roxanne —had spoken truth about me that I myself was completely unaware of. And she was absolutely right. I did need to forgive God....*

I hadn't known Roxanne very long. Less than a year, I think. I had first met with her and her husband when they wanted to publish a book. Over coffee, we did talk business for a while. The two of them were lovely. As one who never really had parents, I found their warmth irresistible and their company, life-giving. And at that first meeting, Roxanne made a comment that disarmed me.

"Lara, I sense some darkness—the darkness of pain—in your soul."

My eyes filled with tears....

"Would you like to come to our home so we can pray for you?" And so began a rich weekly afternoon tradition of prayer, Communion, love, laughter, wisdom, encouragement, and—occasionally—homemade scones.

These two precious souls heard my story not only with their ears, but with their hearts as well. They received with compassion and tears the details about incest at the hands of a military father. Of course I hated my body, the scene of the crime, so to speak. I hated myself. And—unknowingly—I brought into my marriage a three-year-old's perspective on sex: it was a strange activity that definitely did not make me feel loved.

It wasn't until two years into our marriage that all the memories surfaced. Finally the little girl who had been so badly mistreated felt safe enough to share her story. As she did, various parts of my life suddenly made sense.

Why was I always so busy? *Perhaps that was my nature, but my wanting to at least be a moving target for my dad may have fueled my busyness.*

People had asked me, "Why are you always smiling?" *Perhaps that was my nature, but now I saw in those smiles my desperate need to be liked. But maybe it was a "you either laugh or cry" sort of smile.*

Why did grades matter so much to me? *Perhaps being able to succeed in school was in my nature, but those straight As helped me survive. I had purpose and teachers' affirmation.*

Why had I worn that fur-trimmed winter jacket every day *of my freshman year of high school, even when temperatures rose into the high eighties? Perhaps my 100-pound frame needed the extra warmth? No, I was hiding.*

Why, in grad school, did I basically starve myself? *My world was out of control when I was young: I couldn't predict or control my father's behavior. Twenty years later something compelled me to control the one thing in my world I absolutely could: what I ate or didn't eat. So I didn't. I also didn't feel worth spending money on. Any money. Not even for food. And I didn't ever want to be 200 pounds like both of my parents were. And I shudder to think of my father's flesh.*

Yes, Roxanne, you were right to see in my spirit a real darkness. Incest was a soul-shattering violation by a person I thought I could trust, a person I needed to trust. A child who experiences incest has two choices: she can believe she is bad and that's why she's being hurt, or she can believe that her parents are bad, her parents who are all she has to protect her and provide for her. Believing that her parents are bad is much more frightening than believing she is bad. And I easily believed I was bad, and every abusive incident reinforced that conviction. Yes, life was lonely.

As a military kid, I moved around—a lot! Every year between kindergarten and sixth grade, I was at a different school at a different base in a different state. That was my normal—but that "normal" meant not knowing my grandparents or uncles or aunts or cousins. It meant not knowing adults who might have become safe confidants. Yes, life was very lonely. And when the memories came back, I began to understand why I felt that profound loneliness.

Of course, as I put the pieces together, I wrestled with trying to forgive my father for abusing me, derailing my childhood, stealing my innocence, confusing my thoughts about myself—the list goes on and on. I also struggled to forgive my mother for doing nothing to protect me. I don't know how long it took me to get to the point of forgiving them, but it was a matter of years, not months.

For me, the most helpful truth was "hurt people hurt people." I finally reached the point of being able to see my parents as broken people. I didn't know details about their stories. I could guess that his multiple combat assignments damaged my father. I could guess that my mother's mother, with her witchcraft and mysterious ways, might have been the source of much of my mother's brokenness. Hurt people hurt people. With that acknowledgment, I reminded myself, I was not at all excusing their behavior or dismissing the utter evil of my father's actions. But the rage—which, to be honest, I can still too easily plug back in to—was, by God's grace, transformed into a resigned, a reluctant compassion.

But then Roxanne suggested that I needed to forgive God. I had never thought about that! What I had done a lot of, though, was rage at Him. I was relieved to learn at some point that He can handle my anger, that He knew it was there even if I didn't tell Him. He had heard words of my fury: Where were You? Why did You let that happen? That little girl hadn't done anything wrong, yet what happened to her—what You allowed to happen to her—hurt her, harmed her, and felt to her like punishment. And punishment for what? For simply existing? So I'm supposed to feel loved by You? I'm supposed to approach You as my heavenly Father? In light of what my earthly father did to me, thoughts of what You, almighty God and "heavenly Father" could do to me are terrifying!

I still can't sing about God being a "good, good Father." In fact, I'm basically allergic to that metaphor for God. The shepherd metaphor works a bit better for me, but I can't think too much about the wolf He didn't protect me from.

In my calmer moments, I can wryly acknowledge that God's ways are definitely not my ways... and that He doesn't always interfere with someone—even an evil someone—who is exercising his free will. Then I would tell myself that I don't want a God whom I can completely understand because then He wouldn't be a very big God.

But God had allowed the incest to happen. The same God who says His plans for us are plans for good. The same God who promises to be with us always. (If He was with me time after time after time, He hadn't been much help at all.)

Yes, God has done much healing. Thousands of dollars for hundreds of hours of counseling—that was one avenue of His healing power. I have also experienced deliverance from various spirits, the spirit of witchcraft being the most dramatic. And God has used mightily my dear friends who are fervent and faithful pray-ers. I am grateful for God's healing work in my life....

Yet as I've written these words, I've revisited experiences and feelings and questions I usually keep myself too busy to think about. And with this revisiting I've been reminded—or God just reminded me? —that complete healing doesn't always happen this side of heaven. Also, as I retold some of my story here, I've realized I'm still in the process of forgiving God.

It's crazy to see those words—forgiving God—in black and white. After all, C. S. Lewis has compared the distance between us and God to the distance between us and an ant. That this ant needs to forgive

the all-powerful, all-wise, omniscient, omnipresent,
eternal, sovereign God, the Creator of the universe and
the Author of history is preposterous... but real.

If forgiving God means remembering that He is
sovereign, accepting the mystery of His ways, trying to
believe biblical truth about His love for me, and doing
my best to live with Jesus as my Savior and Lord, I am
in the process. And, thankfully, still no lightning.

* * * * *

Do you struggle to forgive? If so, you are among the majority of the women I hear from, teach, and counsel. When I hear about the *actions* they need to forgive, I am very aware that obedience to God's command to forgive will indeed be difficult and costly. Before I say anything more about this command—it is found in the gospels, it is implicit in the Lord's Prayer, and it is echoed in the epistles— let's remember that all of God's commands are for our good. The command to forgive is not an exception.

As you review the list of the actions some women need to forgive, which ones do you most identify with? In addition to categorizing these actions, I've added phrases from the women's sharing. I encourage you to add your specifics in the margins. I want this lesson on forgiveness to be very personal.

Actions for Which We Need to Forgive People—or Ourselves

- Abuse: *being molested, childhood sexual abuse, forgiving ourselves for what happened to us, past sexual assault, incest, being molested at age six, rape, an adult who knew but didn't protect*
- Dysfunctional family: *being raised by alcoholic parent(s), drug abuse, anger, rage, parents' failure to act responsibly, being raised in poverty that could have been avoided*

- Betrayal: *gossip, slander, lying, bullying, backstabbing, judgment, insults, cruel words, jealousy*
- Past mistakes: *overcoming their consequences, shame and guilt, forgiving myself, changing my sinful ways, regret for life choices, blaming others rather than taking responsibility, not letting the past define me*
- Infidelity: *a spouse cheats or has an emotional affair*
- Sabotage: *people who try to prevent success, who spread lies, gossip, and slander women in church or co-workers in Christian businesses trying to undermine, if not destroy, coworkers who are successful*
- Murder: *loved ones were murdered*
- Abortion: *"forgiving myself for having an abortion", "after five years finally coming to terms with the abortion I had", "losing my son at 19 weeks and thinking it was my punishment for having an abortion years before"*
- Death: *natural causes, tragic and unexpected circumstances, no chance to say good-bye, suicide, not overcoming estrangement before the death*
- Self-centeredness: *selfishness, holding grudges, holding on to unforgiveness, choosing not to deal with past hurts*
- Abandonment: *rejection, isolation, "my earthly dad decided to leave our household when I was 12½ years old and go live with my 22-year-old half-sister who was never in my life"*
- Marriage issues: *separation, divorce, custody matters*
- Discrimination: *passed over for promotion, "shunned by clergy because I'm a woman pastor"*
- Sexual harassment *by a boss, coach, teacher, relative, etc.*
- Financial difficulties: *credit card debt, living paycheck to paycheck, student loans, medical bills, etc.*

Precious ones, this list of actions we need to forgive is by no means exhaustive. I hope this list has helped you see that you are not alone.

A list of actions, though, implies the existence of actors or perpetrators. As we consider the *actions* we need to forgive, we actually need to forgive the *people* who took those actions. Who are the people you need to forgive? Again, you can make this exercise more personal by adding the names or initials of the people you need to either forgive or ask to forgive you. Identifying those people now will make the application exercise at the end of the chapter easier.

People We Need to Forgive—Or Ask to Forgive Us

- Ourselves *(I hear this again and again)*
- Parents and stepparents
- Children
- In-laws
- Family members *(siblings, cousins, aunts, uncles, nieces, nephews, grandparents)*
- Spouse/significant other
- Boyfriend
- Friends
- Neighbors
- Coaches
- Acquaintances
- Employer, co-workers, supervisors
- Abusers or offenders, some of whom are dead
- Church members
- Church leaders: *"church leaders who have let me down by living a double standard", "healing from hurts inflicted by fellow Christians in ministry"*
- People who have not asked to be forgiven—and who don't see that they need to be forgiven
- God

In the counseling I've done, I've seen that we struggle most to forgive ourselves and God. I hope that God will use this discussion of His forgiveness to enable us to forgive ourselves and Him as well as everyone else on our list. Seeing a more accurate picture of God, trying to get our mind around how much He loves every single human being, considering all that He has done for us, and entering or enriching the relationship He wants to have with us, we will—by His grace—be better able to extend forgiveness to ourselves as well as to others.

I Understand the Struggle to Forgive...

This topic of forgiveness is a very personal one for me because the process of forgiveness has been the most transformative in my life, second only to inviting Jesus into my heart. Let me explain.

I held on to anger and bitterness for years—many, many years—after the offenses were committed. In fact, one reason I have such a Christ-centered love and am passionate about teaching you about this topic is, I know what it's like to need to forgive others and not be able to do it or, stubbornly, simply not do it. However, one day, by God's grace, I finally responded to the Lord's strong but gentle conviction. Knowing I needed to be changed if I were to forgive, I surrendered to His transforming work. By the power of the Holy Spirit who lives in me as a believer (Ephesians 3:20), the Lord enabled me to forgive a long list of people.

At the time my parents were murdered, I was walking in a life of forgiveness: I was able to extend forgiveness to others because I was very aware and grateful for God's forgiveness of me. I was also intentional about being quick to forgive because I was too familiar with the consequences—the lack of peace, the root of bitterness, the hardened heart—that can come when we don't forgive. However, the murder of my parents tested me to the core. God, however, enabled me to forgive the murderer . . . again… and again… and again. Why *again… and again… and again*? As you yourself may have experienced, different sights, sounds, and thoughts will trigger feelings of anger, hurt, and unforgiveness. When that happens, choose—for your own good, in your own heart and mind, and with the Lord's help—once again to extend forgiveness to the ones who hurt you.

But what exactly *is* forgiveness? I think part of what kept me from forgiving for so many years was, I didn't truly understand what forgiveness is—and isn't. Forgiving is *not* letting your offender off the hook. Forgiving is also *not* excusing the act that hurt you. Forgiveness doesn't mean re-entering a relationship with the person/people you forgive. We don't extend forgiveness only when we're asked to. Forgiveness does not mean they won't ever pay for the injustices done to you.

Dear one, for too long I didn't understand what forgiveness means and doesn't mean. I also didn't realize the benefits and blessings of both receiving God's forgiveness and forgiving others. These are the concepts I want to share with you in this chapter.

God's Forgiveness

Many women have great difficulty believing God has forgiven them, while others embrace the truth that God forgives them when they confess their sins. "If we confess our sins," the apostle John wrote, "[God] who is faithful and just will forgive us our sins and cleanse us from all unrighteousness" (1 John 1:9). Will we choose to believe and act on that promise?

We can too easily doubt the forgiveness God promises. Some of us struggle to remember that Jesus does love us no matter how much we've sinned and no matter how many bad decisions we've made. Yet one woman I heard from is blessed with the confidence all of us can have: "Never think you have fallen too far. God welcomes us back even after we had forgotten about Him."

God is very clear: when we confess our sins, we are forgiven. It ends there. Oh, Satan works hard to remind us of our past sins and to have us doubt God's grace. But God is very clear: He forgives us, and He removes our transgressions from us "as far as the east is from the west" (Psalm 103:12)—and that's far!

And if God forgives us, then who are we to not forgive ourselves? Are we a higher authority than our holy God? Of course not, but in refusing to forgive ourselves, we are being prideful and/or holding ourselves to a higher standard than God does. Dear one, I am guilty of this myself. When I struggle to forgive myself, I go back again and again to Scripture. Yes, all of us are sinners who fall short of God's glory (Romans 3:23). No one is perfect: we all sin, and we all make mistakes—even mistakes that really hurt other people. But God is merciful: not only does He forgive us, but He also brings healing, restores brokenness, and redeems whatever mess we've made.

Will You Let Me Pray for You?

Let's go before our loving Father and ask Him to open our eyes and ears to what He wants us to learn about receiving and resting in His forgiveness of us—and about extending forgiveness to others:

> *Heavenly Father, You know my heart and how urgently I want this precious reader to know forgiveness. I know what it's like to live without Your forgiveness, and I know my own unwillingness to forgive people who sinned against me and hurt me, sometimes deeply. So, Holy Spirit, I ask You to speak through every written word specifically to Your much-loved child who is reading this book.*
>
> *Lord, the topic of forgiveness is challenging. She might want to throw the book out the window. Please work in her heart if she isn't quite ready or willing to forgive. In Your perfect timing and tender way, please open her spirit to receive Your precious gift of forgiveness. Bless her with a biblical understanding of forgiveness, including our need to forgive ourselves. We invite You, Holy Spirit, to teach us through the Word as well as the words in this chapter. In the precious and almighty name of Jesus, we pray. Amen.*

What Is Forgiveness?

The best source for an answer to the question "What is forgiveness?" is the Bible. In fact, by showing me the biblical model of forgiveness, the Lord has enabled me to live with trust in His forgiveness and a willingness to forgive others. That helpful model is the story Jesus told about the unforgiving debtor:

> Then Peter came and said to [Jesus], "Lord, if another member of the church sins against me, how often should I forgive? As many as seven times?" Jesus said to him, "Not seven times, but, I tell you, seventy-seven times.
>
> "For this reason the kingdom of heaven may be compared to a king who wished to settle accounts with his slaves. When he began the reckoning, one who owed him ten thousand talents was brought to him; and, as he could not pay, his lord ordered him to be sold, together with his wife and children and all his possessions, and payment to be made. So the slave fell on his knees before him, saying, 'Have patience with me, and I will pay you everything.' And out of pity for him, the lord of that slave released him and forgave him the debt. But that same slave, as he went out, came upon one of his fellow slaves who owed him a hundred denarii; and seizing him by the throat, he said, 'Pay what you owe.' Then his fellow slave fell down and pleaded with him, 'Have patience with me, and I will pay you.' But he refused; then he went and threw him into prison until he would pay the debt. When his fellow slaves saw what had happened, they were greatly distressed, and they went and reported to their lord all that had taken place. Then his lord summoned him and said to him, 'You wicked slave! I forgave you all that debt because you pleaded with me.

Should you not have had mercy on your fellow slave, as I had mercy on you?' And in anger his lord handed him over to be tortured until he would pay his entire debt. So my heavenly Father will also do to every one of you, if you do not forgive your brother or sister from your heart." — Matthew 18:21-35

So what do we learn from this parable Jesus told?

First, **the forgiveness we extend to others is to be unlimited** (verses 21-22). We aren't, Jesus taught, to forgive only seven times, but seventy-seven times. Yet Jesus wasn't calling us to keep track: He was calling us to, in our heart, be ready to forgive the offender—and then forgive that person again every time our anger and hatred re-emerge in our soul. My need to forgive my parents' murderer required me to forgive again and again and again and again....

Second, **forgiveness is merciful** (verse 33). Showing mercy and compassion, the king forgave a person's huge debt. One talent is equal to about twenty years' wages for a laborer—and this man owed ten thousand talents! That debtor, however, did not extend forgiveness to someone who owed him much, much less. A laborer would be paid a denarius for a day's work, so this debt of 100 denarii amounted to what a worker would make in a little more than three months. The man who received great mercy from the king chooses not to extend any to the one who owes him money.

And what exactly is mercy? *Mercy* is not getting what we deserve. (Grace is getting what we don't deserve. Grace and mercy are often spoken of together.) The Bible is clear that the wages of our sin is our death (Romans 6:23). We don't deserve to be forgiven by our holy God, but when He died in our place, sinless Jesus paid the debt we sinners owed God (Romans 5:8). The man who confessed to murdering my parents does not deserve forgiveness. But neither do I deserve my Lord's forgiveness. Yet because Jesus has forgiven me, I have—by God's grace—forgiven the murderer.

When the king found out that the debtor he had forgiven did not forgive, the king threw the forgiven man into prison. Jesus concluded

His story with these important words: "So my heavenly Father will also do to every one of you, if you do not forgive your brother or sister from your heart" (verse 35). And Jesus' words bring us to the next point.

Third—and as implied in verse 35 and taught in Matthew 6:14-15, Ephesians 4:32, and Mark 11:25—**forgiveness is a command from God**, a command implicit in Jesus' response to His disciples' request to teach them to pray:

> *"Pray then in this way: Our Father in heaven, hallowed be your name. Your kingdom come. Your will be done, on earth as it is in heaven. Give us this day our daily bread. And forgive us our debts, as we also have forgiven our debtors. And do not bring us to the time of trial, but rescue us from the evil one." — Matthew 6:9-13*

Look again at verse 12: we are able to ask God's forgiveness when we ourselves have forgiven those people we need to forgive. For much of my life and in many weekend church services, I just couldn't pray that verse.

And that meant I was living in a spiritual prison, in bondage to people whose evil acts had greatly impacted me—and whom I could not forgive. But then I surrendered to God's command. You see, precious one, God doesn't want us to be in a spiritual prison. He sent Jesus to give us abundant life (John 10:10). Key to that abundant life is living out biblical forgiveness: we are to extend mercy in obedience to Jesus' command to forgive our debtors just as God has forgiven us (Matthew 6:12).

What Forgiveness Means—and Doesn't Mean

I'm quite certain that no one owes you a talent or even a denarius. But someone may have lied to you or cheated on you, cut you off on the freeway, not repaid borrowed money, or committed the horrific crime of rape against you. This list could go on and on. Whatever the actions you need to forgive people for, know that God can help you forgive—for your own good. *Whatever* the person did to you, I encourage you to forgive. No, I don't know the specifics about whom you need to forgive for what, but I do know this: that person/those people are stealing from you right now. You see, your choice to not forgive isn't hurting your betrayers at all. Your choice to not forgive is hurting *you*.

First, trust me when I say that **you don't need to live in bondage** to those who have offended you or hurt you. Jesus gives you the power to cut those offenders loose. In fact, to describe His mission on this earth, Jesus read the following Old Testament words in the synagogue in Nazareth:

> The spirit of the Lord GOD is upon me,
>   because the LORD has anointed me;
> he has sent me to bring good news to the oppressed,
>   to bind up the brokenhearted,
> to proclaim liberty to the captives,
>   and release to the prisoners;
> to proclaim the year of the LORD's favor,
>   and the day of vengeance of our God;
>   to comfort all who mourn. — Isaiah 61:1-2

As you think about these words, picture a heavy chain. Whenever we choose not to forgive, we keep ourselves chained to that person emotionally, spiritually, and mentally. The good news is, Jesus came to set us free. Jesus wants you, precious reader, to live in freedom. You don't need to be chained to anyone. I chose to not be in bondage to my parents' murderer. He had stolen enough from me already, and I was not going to let this evil man be in control of me, my thoughts, my emotions, or my faith in God.

Who, dear one, are you chained to?

Second, **forgiveness means we pray for those who hurt us**. Pray? Yes. Read what Romans 12:14-21 says:

> Bless those who persecute you; bless and do not curse them. Rejoice with those who rejoice, weep with those who weep. Live in harmony with one another; do not be haughty, but associate with the lowly; do not claim to be wiser than you are. Do not repay anyone evil for evil, but take thought for what is noble in the sight of all. If it is possible, so far as it depends on you, live peaceably with all. Beloved, never avenge yourselves, but leave room for the wrath of God; for it is written, "Vengeance is mine, I will repay," says the Lord. "No, if your enemies are hungry, feed them; if they are thirsty, give them something to drink; for by doing this you will heap burning coals on their heads." Do not be overcome by evil, but overcome evil with good.

Precious one, God's ideas about how to treat our enemies are completely opposite the world's view, but—I can testify to this—when we live by God's ideas, we are blessed. To be specific, when I've prayed for my enemies, God has aligned my thoughts with His and given me compassion for them. When I first learned that my parents were murdered, for instance, I felt an overwhelming need to pray. I asked my fellow believers to pray as follows: "O, Lord Jesus, I pray for the assailant(s) to come to know You. Please use this situation as a turning point for the assailant(s). May he/they see it as a call to turn from their wicked ways, receive Your forgiveness, and be transformed by Your love (1 John 1:9; John 3:16). May You redeem this situation by helping the assailant(s) recognize their sin and the gifts of forgiveness and salvation you offer—and then may a radically changed life be a witness for Christ!"

I soon learned that only one assailant was involved in the murder of my parents, John and Maria Elacqua. Thirty-five years old, homeless, with a record of violence and theft, John Miles confessed to the brutal murder of my parents....

John Miles entered my parents' home on October 26, 2005. He knew people were in the house, and he even saw my parents sleeping in their bedroom. However, instead of just leaving, he searched for a knife in the kitchen and then entered my parents' bedroom prepared for a fight and ready to commit murder. John Miles brutally stabbed my mom and dad numerous times. Then, in an effort to clean up the crime scene and cover up the evidence, he spread olive oil on the floor, thinking it was a chemical solution. He confessed thinking he could set the house on fire, but because of nonflammable olive oil being on the floor, the house did not catch fire. (Yes, you just have to chuckle at the idea of trying to light a house on fire using olive oil.) John Miles then took my mom's body, stuffed her in the trunk of her car, and then abandoned her, the car, and some of his clothes near a vacant building. He stole valuable and sentimental items from my parents' home and then dumped them in an undisclosed location. The items were never recovered.

I had planned to give John Miles a Bible once the trial was over. I wanted to write him a note explaining the salvation story and telling him that I forgave him for murdering my parents. I never had the opportunity, though. Approximately five months after John Miles took my parents' lives, he took his own. On March 25, 2006, John Miles committed suicide in his jail cell—and I wept for this man who died without knowing the love and forgiveness of Christ. And, dear friend, I believe that because I prayed for John Miles—even before I knew his name—I was able to shed tears of sincere grief for the man who murdered my parents.

Third, **we are to forgive even when the offender doesn't ask to be forgiven**. Remember when Jesus was hanging on the cross? Jesus had never sinned, but He became sin by taking on our sin (2 Corinthians 5:21), and then He died, a sacrifice for our sin, so that we can be forgiven for our sins—past, present, and future. As Jesus bore our every sin, His very last words were "Father, forgive them; for they do not know what they are doing" (Luke 23:34).

"Father, forgive them"? Jesus had endured false accusations, a trial in an illegal kangaroo court, a judgment of guilt, abandonment by His closest friends, rejection by people He came to save, ridicule, mockery, the crowd's taunts, the soldiers' spit, an almost-deadly flogging, a crown of thorns shoved onto His head, nails hammered into His hands and feet, the excruciatingly painful death by crucifixion, and the humiliation of hanging on a cross, yet Jesus said, "Father, forgive them"! I don't know about you, dear reader, but after experiencing a dishonest justice system, rejection and abandonment by those I love, life-threatening physical abuse, the emotional torture of people's cruelty and lies, and weakness due to blood loss, sleeplessness, and hunger, I don't think I'd be saying, "Father, forgive them"! But Jesus did. So, if we follow Jesus' example, we forgive people even when they haven't asked to be forgiven. (John Miles included an apology in his confession statement, but even if he hadn't, I had already decided in my heart that I would forgive him.)

Also, I shared in the first chapter that I had been molested. To this day, he has not apologized, but—by God's grace—I have forgiven him. To model biblical forgiveness for my family members, most of whom don't walk closely with Jesus, I even asked him to be in my wedding. He said yes, and his participation transformed him from outcast to family. And his experience illustrates what Jesus does for us: We sinners were outcasts, enemies of Christ, yet Jesus died for us. By doing so, He made available to us forgiveness for our sins, reconciliation with God the Father, and the opportunity to become a member of God's family. We are no longer outcasts, but children of the living God.

Back, though, to the unapologetic abuser. Someone's failure to apologize to me will not impact my relationship with Christ. Yet I put myself in bondage to that person if I wait for an apology that may never come. In some cases, the abuser might even be dead, and an apology will definitely never come. But, dear one, don't let the absence of an apology rob you of the freedom that will be yours when you choose to forgive your offenders even when they don't ask to be forgiven.

Fourth, **forgiveness does not make the offense okay. Forgiveness makes *you* okay.** Whatever wrongs have been done to you will *always* be wrong—and let me reassure you that forgiving people doesn't make what they did all right. Your forgiveness of the offender does not minimize the pain, excuse the damage, or make the act acceptable. Instead, your forgiveness will make *you* all right. No longer will your lack of forgiveness interfere with your relationship with Jesus or eat away at your insides. God commands forgiveness for the benefit of the forgiver.

Now—and I feel very strongly about this—when someone asks you to forgive them, you may respond with "I forgive you." That's fine—but never, ever, dear one, respond with "That's okay." What was done to you is absolutely *not* okay! That offense will always be an offense. A sin will always be a sin. Forgiveness doesn't change that!

Of course my parents' murder and the sexual abuse I experienced will always be wrong, but we don't always have to carry the heavy weight of our unforgiveness. We have Jesus' invitation to exchange our heavy burden for His light burden:

> "Come to me, all you that are weary and are carrying heavy burdens, and I will give you rest. Take my yoke upon you, and learn from me; for I am gentle and humble in heart, and you will find rest for your souls. For my yoke is easy, and my burden is light." — Matthew 11:28-30

When we forgive someone, we are in a sense entrusting that person to God's judgment. We can forgive because we can trust our righteous God's statement that vengeance belongs to Him: "I will repay" (Romans 12:19). We can be at peace and walk in freedom, no longer burdened by unforgiveness.

Fifth, **forgiveness doesn't mean you forget what happened**—and God doesn't ask us to forget. In fact, forgetting may actually place us at risk for further injury. I would, for example, be foolish to forget what the abusive family member did to me. I am still in contact with him, and I see him when I travel to my birthplace and my home for many years. Whenever I visit this relative, I do let him be around my children, but he is not allowed to touch them. This boundary is a bit difficult to enforce in an Italian family that greets people with hugs and kisses! Nevertheless, I set this boundary at the very beginning of his relationship with my children. First in writing and then in person, I was very specific and direct: "You may speak to, but you may *never* touch my children." And I clearly remember how he tested me by extending his index finger so that my baby could grab it. I immediately slapped his hand and told him to follow me. In the privacy of one of the bedrooms, I reiterated that I was not going to allow him to be around my girls if he was going to ignore the boundaries I had established.

In addition to establishing and enforcing boundaries, I've taught my children about sexual abuse and precautions to take. They also know the difference between good touch and bad touch. As my daughters grew more mature and were able to understand more, I gave them additional information about how to protect themselves—and I told them more about my own story. My precious girls even know the exact person I'm referring to. I have never allowed this family member to be alone with my children—and I never will.

Dear one, for your own good, God wants you to forgive those people who have hurt you, but forgiving does not mean forgetting. If you choose to maintain a relationship with the abuser, you absolutely need to establish wise and firm boundaries—and then always enforce them vigilantly. Know, however, that you don't ever have to choose to be in relationship with your abuser. Forgiveness does not require re-establishing the relationship.

Some Blessings of Forgiving and Being Forgiven

God has blessings for us when we accept His forgiveness, when we receive forgiveness from people we have hurt, and when we forgive people who have hurt us. What follows is not an exhaustive list, but what is here may encourage you to ask for, receive, and extend forgiveness.

First, **Jesus Christ came to give us abundant life**. He said as much: "The thief comes only to steal and kill and destroy. I came that they may have life, and have it abundantly" (John 10:10). Dear one, know that I am not saying the abundant life means guaranteed wealth and health. No! The abundant life Jesus promises refers to our being in relationship with Him, and He has given you and me every spiritual blessing we need in this life on earth as well as the ultimate spiritual blessing of spending eternity with Him (Ephesians 1:3). God may bless you with wealth and health, but the true abundance Jesus promised is neither physical nor material blessings. Jesus knows that truly abundant life is the spiritual blessing of living our earthly life in relationship with Him.

Second, **the Lord wants you to live in peace**. Consider the benedictions we find in the Bible:

> The peace of God, which surpasses all understanding,
> will guard your hearts and your minds in Christ Jesus.
> — Philippians 4:7

> May the God of hope fill you with all joy and peace
> in believing, so that you may abound in hope by the
> power of the Holy Spirit. — Romans 15:13

> Those of steadfast mind you keep in peace—
> in peace because they trust in you. — Isaiah 26:3

Only our gracious and loving Lord can give us peace beyond our comprehension in circumstances that call for panic, fear, worry—for anything but peace. Also, there is no wound, my dear one, that God cannot heal, and there is no emotion that He cannot replace with peace.

Third, **God wants you to know freedom**. As we've seen in this passage, Jesus came to give us freedom:

> [The Lord GOD] has sent [Jesus]...
> to proclaim liberty to the captives,
>   and release to the prisoners. — Isaiah 61:1-2

Fourth, **joy comes when we choose to forgive**. You just read these words, but they are worth reading again:

> May the God of hope fill you with all joy and peace
> in believing, so that you may abound in hope by the
> power of the Holy Spirit. — Romans 15:13

Who doesn't want to experience abundant life, peace, freedom, and joy? Forgiving others is a sure path toward those blessings.

PERSONAL REFECTION AND APPLICATION

Did the incident happen one year ago, five years ago, or twenty years ago? How heavy is the burden of bitterness, anger, and hate you may still be carrying around? Whenever the pain was inflicted on you and however much the burden of unforgiveness weighs, I hope I've been clear: forgiveness is for *your* benefit. So—I can't encourage you enough—don't allow the offenders to have power or influence over you any longer! Regardless of how long it's been since the offense, if you choose not to forgive, the hurts from your past will continue to impact you and your daily life. Too many women have learned the hard way that their failure to both deal with the hurt and forgive those who hurt them leads them down the road of destruction. These women have often been consumed with bitterness and anger—and then turned to false gods (e.g., drugs, alcohol, materialism, sex) to try to dull the pain. I don't want their story to be yours.

So please spend some time working on the five application points below. I have prayed that God will use the truths in this chapter to free you and to transform your life. May you finish this chapter 100 pounds lighter because you've shed the burden you carried when you first opened this book. Choose to live a life of forgiveness—that's the best way ever to lose unwanted weight!

1. Read 1 John 1:9. Take some time to be with the Lord and confess your sins. Also, ask Him to reveal those sins that you are either blind to or comfortable with. Then linger with Him so you don't miss His response.

2. Who do you need to forgive and for what? Any notes you wrote at the beginning of this chapter may help you answer this question.

3. Read Matthew 11:28-30. Now comes the step of going to the Lord and exchanging your heavy burden of unforgiveness for His rest and a much lighter burden. Choosing to trust that God will judge justly those who hurt you, lay your pain at His feet. Unburden yourself of all the emotions, all the details from all the incidents, and all the reasons you don't want to forgive. Lay all that down.

4. Review these Scriptures: Ephesians 3:20; Mark 9:23; Jeremiah 32:17; Philippians 2:13; Galatians 2:20; 2 Corinthians 5:17; and Ephesians 2:10. Then pray and ask God to—by the power of the Holy Spirit—give you the ability to forgive the people you listed above.

5. What can you do to stay free of unforgiveness? I have a couple ideas for you.

   • Every morning put on the whole armor of God (Ephesians 6:10-17).
   • Believe God is who He says He is. In Exodus 34:6 God described Himself as "a God merciful and gracious, slow to anger, and abounding in steadfast love and faithfulness."

- Live in the truth of who God says you are. His witness, His servant, His chosen one, His beloved, His adopted child!

I want to say more about who our God is and why He chose us. First, I'll address the question with the short answer. God chose us so that we may know Him and believe in Him. The Hebrew word for "know" is *yada*, and it means "to perceive and see, find out and discern, to have knowledge, or be acquainted with." To be specific, we can be in relationship with God: we can perceive His presence with us, discern His guidance, know His truth, and be intimately related to Him who is Creator, Sustainer, King of Kings, Sovereign, and Lord; who is all-powerful, all-knowing, and everywhere present; who has existed throughout eternity past and will exist throughout eternity future; who proclaims, "I am the Alpha and the Omega, the first and the last, the beginning and the end" (Revelation 22:13).

Precious one, when you choose to be in relationship with God by naming His Son your Savior and Lord and when you choose to read and study His Word, you can know Him in a rich, life-giving way. The better you know who God is, the more easily you will trust His character and believe His promises.

That said, I still don't understand—and probably never will this side of heaven—why I have experienced such horrific tragedies. I don't have answers to all my questions about my parents' murder, my dysfunctional family and abusive childhood, the death of my baby Rachel, the loss of a job, having a special needs child, etc., but I trust God. And because I know Him, I can trust Him even when I don't have the answers I'd like to have.

I am also able to say that God is good even though all the good things I'd like to experience haven't happened to me. Yet my knowledge of God and His goodness enables me—and I hope it enables you too—to walk by faith, not by sight (2 Corinthians 5:7). When we know God—and when we are always getting to know Him better—we live with faith: we live trusting Him even when we don't understand Him or His ways. For those who believe that

Jesus is God's one and only Son sent to pay the penalty and die for our sins, God provides forgiveness and eternal life. May we receive and celebrate the abundant life of peace, freedom, and joy that Jesus so generously gives to those of us whom He forgives and whom He enables to forgive others.

PRAYER: *Almighty God, I thank You that You allowed Your Son, Jesus Christ—who knew no sin (2 Corinthians 5:21)—to take on not only my sin, but also my offender's sin, so we who believe that Jesus is Your Son and that He did rise from the dead can be in a right relationship with You.*

Grateful for Your forgiveness, I do confess my sin to You. For starters, please forgive me for my unforgiving heart. I also ask Your forgiveness for... Thank You for forgiving me. Thank You, too, for the gift of Your Spirit living in me and empowering me to do what You call and command me to do. You have forgiven me for so much. Please enable me to forgive again and again and again those who have sinned against me.

CHAPTER **SIX**

The Church and Its Resources

MORE THAN 1,100 WOMEN responded to the survey for this book. Imagine how different their personalities and their stories are. Despite that wide variety, these women consistently said that being active in a Bible-based church helped them persevere through their pain, facilitated their healing, and introduced them to a life of freedom.

Now wait just a minute! Please don't put the book down or throw it across the room! I recognize that you may not attend church. Or perhaps your church attendance is sporadic. Maybe you attend church only on Easter and Christmas. Maybe you've seen the hypocrisy of church members and simply don't want any part of organized religion. Or—as some women shared with me—people in the church have hurt you deeply, so of course you ask, *Why would I want to spend my precious time at church?* Let me try to answer that question by sharing my story. Perhaps your story is similar to mine:

I grew up Roman Catholic. That meant I attended mass every Saturday at 4:00 p.m. I knew when to stand, when to sit, and when to kneel. I knew when to recite words I didn't understand, but I had them memorized. So, on cue, I joined in the congregation's monotone response to the priest's statements. As a good Catholic girl, I also attended Catholic school from kindergarten until eighth grade and confirmation classes when I was in high school. I was baptized as an infant, I was confirmed in the Catholic Church as a teenager, and all the while I didn't understand what I was saying or what commitment I was making. I was merely going through the motions and checking off a box. I was spiritually dead.

Some women will say they grew up Catholic or Protestant. Usually that means they were just going through the motions, often without understanding what exactly they were doing or why—and that still happens today. Perhaps these women were in church because it kept things calm at home or, later, because it was good for business. And sometimes going to church is a cultural expectation (think "Bible Belt").

Friend, God wants you to be a part of a vibrant church that teaches the whole counsel of God and offers you a community where you are loved and accepted. Allow me to show you what I mean by *church* and why I believe you would benefit by being involved in a church as you navigate life's pain on the way to a life of freedom.

When I was in graduate school, two new friends invested in me. They shared with me the gospel message—the good news that God the Father loves me so much that He sent His one and only Son, Jesus, to die on the cross for my sins. By putting my faith in this Son, I would receive forgiveness of my sins and eternal life. I was open to that truth because I was beginning to realize that all this world could offer me was not enough—and would never be enough. So I acknowledged before the Lord that I am a sinner. I knew from the Bible that the wages of sin is death, meaning eternal separation from God. I also knew that I could never do enough good things to make me worthy of entering heaven. The chasm between sinful me and holy God can only be bridged by my relationship with Jesus Christ. When I believe that Jesus—who was fully God and fully man— died on the cross for my sins, I am able to enter into a relationship with Him.

So, dear one, as I've mentioned throughout this book, an essential and foundational step to living in freedom is your relationship with Jesus Christ. You and I aren't able to live in freedom without acknowledging our sins, recognizing that Jesus bore the consequences for our sins, and naming Him as our Lord and Savior. If you haven't yet taken this life-changing step, please refer to "The Invitation to Know Christ" on page 16. One more thing. As with any relationship, your relationship with Jesus can only be maintained if you spend time with Him, learn more about Him, and get to know Him better.

After I became a Christian, I started going to a nondenominational Protestant church that the two friends who introduced me to Jesus attended. There I met other like-minded Christians who wanted to learn more about Jesus, and we did so through Bible studies and the pastor's sermons.

But just because the building is called a church or just because someone who calls himself a pastor, reverend, or priest speaks from the front of the room doesn't necessarily mean you've found a healthy and vibrant church community where people are becoming more like Jesus. Through the years I have counseled many people who aren't attending Bible-believing, Bible-teaching churches. As a result, they aren't growing in their relationship with the Lord. They might attend church every week, but spiritual growth and transformation into Christlikeness aren't happening.

So how do we find a healthy church where we can grow in our knowledge of and love for Jesus? The Bible identifies at least five key qualities that can help us determine whether a specific church will help us become all God calls us to be.

1. A healthy church clearly states what it believes, and what it believes is consistent with what the Bible teaches (2 Timothy 4:1-5). Unfortunately, beloved, people around the world who call themselves "Christians" are not submitting to sound biblical doctrine. Instead they are seeking after false teachers who say whatever the crowd wants to hear and who include their personal and unbiblical ideas and opinions. Many people will settle for churches that don't teach truth, and I have several thoughts about why that happens.

Sometimes, for instance, I don't think some people even realize they are settling. New believers may not yet know Scripture well enough to recognize false teaching—and the Lord clearly tells us in Scripture that people will be attracted to teachers who tell them what they want to hear or what is easy to hear. If a pastor's messages don't ever prompt soul-searching, call us to repentance, or help us recognize we need to make some changes, what's not to like about those sermons whether you're a new or a long-time believer? We all like to feel good about ourselves, and teaching that is no longer biblically sound lets us continue to follow our own desires. Then, since we all desire the validation that comes when we associate with like-minded people, we stay at the church even though God's truth is not preached or taught.

The list of why people stay under false teachers continues. People, for example, tend to like a god who looks, thinks, and acts like them, a god they don't have to submit to, a god who allows them to live life their way. Oh, it's easy enough to say the words, "I'm submitting to Jesus as my Lord and Savior" because who wants to go to hell? But

⌐ TINA C. ELACQUA, PH.D. ⌐

besides being our Savior, Jesus is to be our Lord and the King over us. We—who like to rule our own life—are to place Jesus in His rightful position as the Authority and Ruler in our life. When we acknowledge Jesus as Lord, we are also to exchange *our* will for His will. We are saying, "Lord, You know better than I do, and I want to follow Your lead." And every day—sometimes every hour of every day—we need to again make this choice to do life His way, not ours. We say, "I will surrender every aspect of my life to You, Lord, and I ask You to transform my life and me personally so that I live in line with Your truth." Only with that choice and the help of the Holy Spirit can we live a transformed life characterized by purpose, joy, and peace.

I hope you now understand more clearly why I encourage you to search diligently for a church with a belief statement that is completely consistent with what the Bible teaches. A healthy church will not waver from biblical doctrine. It stays true to what God teaches and what He requires rather than be blown about by the ever-changing ways of the world or by their own efforts to appeal to the contemporary nonbeliever. Instead, a healthy church will—with love and compassion—stand firm on its core Christian beliefs and teach them clearly and faithfully (1 Thessalonians 3:7-8).

Know, too, that a church can communicate its beliefs in a variety of ways. The belief statement may be on their website, but that's only a start. Those beliefs should be taught from the pulpit and—most important—lived out by the members. The church I attend also offers classes where a member of the pastoral staff introduces our core beliefs, and then the people in the class are able to ask whatever questions they have. If those attending the class agree with the church's belief statements, they are free to join the church. Realize, that church membership doesn't mean you're automatically saved. Only a relationship with Jesus Christ can provide salvation. Yet I can't encourage you enough: Once you have named Jesus your Savior and Lord, find a healthy church that will enable you to stand firm on biblical truth and neither succumb to the world's temptations nor follow the world's teachings.

2. A healthy church has pastors who preach the Bible (Acts 2:37-42). In His grace, God has given us the Bible as the primary means by which we are able to learn more about Jesus and how we are to act as His followers. A healthy church also teaches the congregation spiritual disciplines such as learning to read, study, and understand the Bible as well as praying, meditating on Scripture, and memorizing passages from God's Word. A healthy church will definitely equip the congregation with the tools they need to maintain their relationship with the Lord by spending time with Him, talking to Him, listening for His voice, and obeying His commands.

That said, don't think that because you already know how to study God's Word on your own, you don't need to have a home church or attend a weekly worship service. Yet Sunday mornings should not be our only time with the Lord. Neither should Sunday mornings be the only time we spend with fellow believers.

3. A healthy church encourages members to use their gifts and talents for the benefit of the body of Christ (Ephesians 4:11-16) and to fulfill the Great Commission (Matthew 28:18-20). Rather than merely being spectators at a worship service, we are to be active and engaged participants. Rather than watching others sing to the Lord or just going through the motions, we are to worship God with our heart and mind as well as our voice. We are to engage with the content of the sermon, seek to understand it, and work to apply the truth we learn to our everyday life. Ideally, we leave the service not feeling as though it was simply a pleasant experience, but aware that we are changed because we spent time with the Lord. Also, as we leave the service, we are to be focused on other people and willing to help meet the needs of the congregation, the community, and even people on the other side of the globe.

In addition, we are to identify the spiritual gifts the Lord has given us and use them as He intends us to: for the benefit of the body. Are you gifted as a teacher? Then teach—preschoolers or adults, elementary or high school. Do you have the gift of hospitality? Open your home to a Bible study. Take meals to new moms. Are you a skilled administrator? Offer the church your services on a volunteer basis. Maybe you're gifted in prayer. If so, establish a new avenue for church members to pray, or meet weekly with like-minded pray-ers to pray for your church. Finally, are you gifted at sharing the gospel? If so, share it—and thereby fulfill the Great Commission, God's command to "make disciples of all nations" by sharing the news of Jesus' love and forgiveness (Matthew 28:19).

4. A healthy church sees people proclaiming their faith in Jesus for the first time (Acts 2:41, 47; 9:31). Yes, we want a church that grows in numbers, but a church with 10,000 members is not necessarily any healthier than a church of 500 members. A healthy church will have attendees finding Christ, being baptized, and then growing toward spiritual maturity. We want people who are growing in their relationship with the Lord, maturing in their knowledge of their Savior, and reflecting more clearly the presence of Jesus Christ within them (Ephesians 4:13; 5:1).

5. A healthy church follows the Bible's guidelines for church discipline (Matthew 18:15-20). Anytime a church is made up of more than one member, conflict is unavoidable. We are unique individuals, made in the image of God yet having personal tastes and a sin nature. So the question is not "Will we have conflict?" but "When we have conflict, how will we resolve it?" Before committing to a church, learn whether the church leadership as well as individuals in the congregation follow the Matthew 18 process for resolving conflicts.

Now, although it isn't exactly a matter of church discipline, the Bible also instructs us to confess our sins to one another (Proverbs 28:13; Mark 1:5). With love and compassion—and very aware of our own sins—we are to help loved ones recognize their sin (Matthew 7:1-5). And the reason we confess our sins to one another and, at other times, help others acknowledge their sin is always reconciliation to one another and to the Lord. Greater unity results as we encourage each other to forsake our sin and become more like Jesus. When prayer requests are shared, they are never to fuel gossip and slander.

Instead, those heartfelt requests are opportunities to lift up hurting brothers and sisters to the One who can heal them, free them, and make them more like Jesus.

A Safe Place

A church that qualifies as a healthy place of worship has as its foundation the commitment to live according to the truth found in the Bible. Unfortunately, as the women who completed my survey shared, time and time again, that the church was not a safe place with leaders who helped them heal. Some women did not think they could talk about their pain and its causes, especially when—and this happens—the church has caused or is contributing to their pain.

If a woman is to feel safe at a church, a focus on God's Word—on its being both taught and lived out—is essential. The body of Christ needs to *be* Jesus to the hurting. Jesus esteemed women, He considered women co-heirs in God's kingdom, and He provided a safe place for those who were struggling. Likewise, the church should be a haven that offers the brokenhearted practical resources and Christlike support. Many churches, for instance, offer divorce care (classes, support groups, and designated pastoral counselors on staff). Many churches also have Bible studies on such life issues as how to be a good steward of finances, how to study the Bible, and how to walk through grief and loss. More specifically, when you choose a church, be sure that people in that church not only encourage you to sit in the ashes before the Lord and process your pain, but are also willing to sit with you as you do so. As we think back to chapter 2, we don't need people around us who act like Job's accusatory friends. Instead, we need to be intentional about surrounding ourselves with people who treat the wounded with compassion and tenderness just as Jesus Himself did.

Let's review a few scriptures that reflect the heart of the Lord and, ideally, of a church that chooses to emulate Jesus:

Soon afterwards [Jesus] went on through cities and villages, proclaiming and bringing the good news of the kingdom of God. The twelve were with him, as well as some women who had been cured of evil spirits and infirmities. – Luke 8:1-2

Now when Jesus returned, the crowd welcomed him, for they were all waiting for him. Just then there came a man named Jairus, a leader of the synagogue. He fell at Jesus' feet and begged him to come to his house, for he had an only daughter, about twelve years old, who was dying.

As he went, the crowds pressed in on him. Now there was a woman who had been suffering from hemorrhages for twelve years; and though she had spent all she had on physicians, no one could cure her. She came up behind him and touched the fringe of his clothes, and immediately her hemorrhage stopped. Then Jesus asked, "Who touched me?" When all denied it, Peter said, "Master, the crowds surround you and press in on you." But Jesus said, "Someone touched me; for I noticed that power had gone out from me." When the woman saw that she could not remain hidden, she came trembling; and falling down before him, she declared in the presence of all the people why she had touched him, and how she had been immediately healed. He said to her, "Daughter, your faith has made you well; go in peace."

While he was still speaking, someone came from the leader's house to say, "Your daughter is dead; do not trouble the teacher any longer." When Jesus heard this, he replied, "Do not fear. Only believe, and she will be saved." When he came to the house, he did not allow anyone to enter with him, except Peter, John, and James, and the child's father and mother. They were all weeping and wailing for her; but he said, "Do not weep; for she is not dead but sleeping." And they laughed at him, knowing that she was dead. But he took her by the hand and called out, "Child, get up!" Her spirit returned, and she got up at once. Then he directed them to give her something to eat. Her parents were astounded; but he ordered them to tell no one what had happened. – Luke 8:40-56

Now [Jesus] was teaching in one of the synagogues on the Sabbath. And just then there appeared a woman with a spirit that had crippled her for eighteen years. She was bent over and was quite unable to stand up straight. When Jesus saw her, he called her over and said, "Woman, you are set free from your ailment." When he laid his hands on her, immediately she stood up straight and began praising God. – Luke 13:10-13

Each of these passages—and please know I could have provided many more examples—reflect the heart of Jesus, a Man who respected women. Jesus' attitude toward and His interaction with women were radical in His day. He genuinely valued women in a culture that considered them second-class citizens. Yet Jesus showed His high regard for women by spending significant time with them, healing them, ministering to them, and allowing them to both travel with Him and learn alongside men as He preached the good news of the kingdom of God.

In light of how Jesus treated women, dear one, I encourage you to earnestly look for a church that respects women just as He did. Look for a church that supports you when you need to grieve, rage at God, and sit in the ashes—steps we take in order to one day truly experience living in freedom. Keep looking until you find a church community of people who willingly walk with the wounded and who are thereby channels of God's healing love and peace. Tiffany, my friend and sister in Christ, found such a church. You can read some of her story below as she shares her journey toward living in freedom, a journey she successfully completed thanks to the support of a healthy church.

> I was seven months pregnant with our first child when I found out....
>
> The first seven years of our marriage had been less than ideal. We were two separate people living together, but we were not living as one. However, during the previous two years, we had been doing really well. The reason was, we had both accepted Christ, and we had moved beyond being Christian by culture to actually pursuing a relationship with the Lord. We were also working to create a marriage that reflected the kingdom of heaven.
>
> So I was seven months pregnant when I found out something I hadn't known about. That in itself wasn't unusual. For the first eight years of our marriage, I was always learning something more about the man I married. Things that had happened before he met me. His childhood abuse by a neighborhood boy and later by a scoutmaster. College indiscretions. His tumultuous relationship with his father that eventually faded into no relationship at all. All these experiences had strong, negative effects on my husband and therefore on our marriage. They caused distance between us, and I often felt isolated. After all, I had moved into his world, filled with his friends and his family (my family lived two hours away). As my husband's stories came out over time, I felt more and more alone. These little secrets that he shared with me as he became more confident of my love for him had a big impact on me.
>
> I was seven months pregnant when I found out yet another secret....
>
> When we became Christians, everything changed. We had a new circle of friends—and they were our

*friends, not just his friends. Everything about our life
was different, was better. I felt like we had finally made
our marriage a priority, and we were growing as a
couple. We were also active in a church. My husband
was the worship leader there. And, finally, after eight
years of marriage, we were expecting a baby.*

*So I was seven months pregnant when my husband
got a horrible, ugly brown envelope in the mail. He
burned it and then told me it had pornography in it.
An aspect of my husband's previous life had caught up
with him. The enemy was attacking.*

*Deciding that I'd had enough of this slow trickle
of secrets, I told him the next day that I wanted to
know everything. I was tired of feeling anxious, always
expecting him to share yet another secret. I always felt
like I was standing on a cliff and that his next secret
was going to send me over the edge. I didn't want to
keep being surprised. I just wanted the entire story.*

*So, my husband of eight years took a deep breath
and told me. My husband—who was about to become
a father—looked me in the eye and confessed what he
had promised himself he would never tell me: he had
been unfaithful to me during the first several years of
our marriage. I don't know what I expected to hear
from him as he told me the whole story, but it certainly
was not that.*

*Hearing what he said helped me understand why
I had felt so isolated and distanced from him in those
early years of our marriage. I realized that the times I
was alone, he had been with someone else—and I never
dreamed that was happening. I had heard somewhere
that the partner always has some idea that an affair
is happening. I honestly had no clue. We'd made vows
to each other, and we had promised each other that
divorce would never be an option for us. We were both*

children of divorce, and we never intended to see divorce as a solution to our problems. Yet a part of me always thought that infidelity might be a reason to break that promise, and now I faced that exact decision.

As I heard my husband's words, I was hurt beyond anything I had ever felt before. I was angry. I was in shock. I didn't want to believe it, but the heartbreak kept me rooted in that excruciating reality. "Lord, why? Why did he do this? How could he?" As I screamed these silent questions and cried as I'd never cried before, the Lord began His work.

I can't even begin to describe the feelings the Lord began to plant in my heart. I was so grateful for the total peace He gave me. He also gave me the ability to forgive my husband. That only happened because the Lord worked in my heart. In fact, the moment my husband told me what he had done, I forgave him. The Spirit immediately reminded me that my husband was not the same man I had married. He was different because he had found Christ. He was invested in our marriage. He was invested in our faith. He was excited about becoming a father. He was changed. God had given him a new heart.

Yes, the Holy Spirit was definitely working in me. I never could have forgiven him on my own—and, always with tears, I had to forgive him again and again as I cried for the next two months. I cried while we registered for baby gifts. I cried when I told my closest friends. I cried through church services. I forgave my husband because he was repentant and because he had changed. Still, I cried—and forgave again. My husband spent the next several years proving to me he was not the same person who had cheated on me.

Looking back, I can't imagine having gone through that—and staying married—if God had not surrounded us with an amazing church family. We had gone from attending Sunday services once or twice a month to being all in. We were involved in Bible studies that served as accountability groups. And when I needed them most, the members of my women's group surrounded me physically, emotionally, and prayerfully. I received daily phone calls and visits. When I was put on bed rest with preeclampsia, I had these dear friends bring in meals and then sit and talk with me. My husband's small group—many of them the husbands of my friends—did the same for him.

Two months after my husband shared with me his secret, our first child was born. A beautiful baby girl.

My husband worked hard to regain my trust. For a long time, whenever he headed out, I asked where he was going, who he was going to be with, and how long he was going to be gone. He always answered my questions. He also called if he was going to be later than he'd said he was. He never complained. He simply did what I needed him to do. He held me when I cried. He apologized and continued to prove that I could trust him. And we prayed. I read my Bible and continued to grow closer to the Lord.

My mind was filled with thoughts like these: Jesus died for my sins. He died for my husband's sins. My sins are enough to condemn me. All sin separates us from God. We human beings rank order sin, deciding that one sin is worse than another. But from our holy God's perspective, sin is sin. All of it separates us from our heavenly Father. Romans 3:23 says, "All have sinned and fall short of the glory of God." But Jesus died for my sins; He also died for my husband's sins. In light of the fact that Jesus forgave me, I am called to forgive even a cheating husband.

More than twenty years later, we are still together. We have five beautiful children. We are best friends. Together we serve the Lord by running a nonprofit that plants churches. I cannot imagine life without my husband. It took a few years for him to regain my trust. Truthfully, from time to time, the enemy still tries to use this situation like a wedge between us. And when my husband is running late, I will occasionally wonder what he is doing and who he is with. But then I remind myself—I'm sure it's a Holy Spirit nudge—that I have forgiven him and that he hasn't given me any reason to doubt his faithfulness since the day he confessed.

God requires all of us to ask Him for forgiveness and to repent, to turn away from our sins. My husband did that. My husband also asked for my forgiveness, and I have forgiven him. By doing so, I was allowing the Holy Spirit to work through me to do in my heart what I could not do on my own. And through His church, God gave me people to walk with me, grieve with me, and pray for me.

PERSONAL REFLECTION AND APPLICATION

1. Are you actively involved in a church? If not, after reading this chapter and seeing the importance of being actively engaged in a healthy church, consider the value of being part of a church body. What is keeping you from getting involved? Right now spend some time asking the Lord to show you what is keeping you from finding and being part of a vibrant God-fearing congregation.

2. If you do attend church, evaluate your church according to the five key qualities described in this chapter:
   - How well does your church clearly state what it believes? To what degree are the belief statements consistent with what the Bible teaches?

- Does your church have pastors who preach the Bible?
- Does your church encourage members to use their gifts and talents for the benefit of the body of Christ? Does your church encourage members to use their gifts and talents to fulfill the Great Commission? In what ways are you using your gifts to serve the body? To obey Jesus' Great Commission?
- Is your church seeing more and more people proclaim their faith in Jesus for the first time?
- Does your church follow the Bible's Matthew 18 guidelines for church discipline?

3. To what extent is your church a safe place? Are you able to remove your mask and sit in your dark places with sisters and brothers in Christ? Are you encouraged to walk alongside fellow believers who have endured great pain? What parts of Tiffany's story encourage you to first become healthier and then to help others?

PRAYER: Lord Jesus, You are the only One who can heal my heart. Only You can repair the broken places. I realize that You often do that miraculous work in the context of a vibrant church community. Help me, Lord, to find a church where I am taught Your Word, able to grow spiritually with fellow believers, encouraged to use my gifts for Your glory, and allowed to be genuine and transparent. Please use me to comfort others with the same comfort You have given me. In the name of Jesus, my Healer and Redeemer, my Savior and Friend, I pray. Amen.

Praise be to the God and Father of our Lord Jesus Christ, the Father of compassion and the God of all comfort, who comforts us in all our troubles, so that we can comfort those in any trouble with the comfort we ourselves have received from God. — 2 Corinthians 1:3-4 (NIV)

CHAPTER **SEVEN**

The Life-Giving Support of a Christian Community

SARAH SHARES HER STORY here...

I was sitting in the back seat of Stephanie's van. We were heading home from the retreat with a passenger who hadn't ridden with us earlier. When she asked me a question, I wanted to tell her about David, so I started from the top. I'd had a normal pregnancy and brought home a healthy baby boy, and he died from SIDS when he was 12 weeks old.

From the driver's seat, Stephanie quickly glanced at me in the rearview mirror and said, "Sarah, can you tell us more about David? What was he like? What did he look like? What was your favorite time with him?"

I paused and teared up. It meant so much to me that Stephanie would nudge me to go deeper. She knows that healing comes from being vulnerable with people who are genuinely invested in their friendship with you. I've learned I don't have to give my heart away to everyone I meet, but at certain times when we share the hard parts of our story, God's glory really shines through.

That's how my friendship with Stephanie had started: awhile back I had reminded her it was OK to go deeper.

***

After David died, I remember sitting in the office where I worked and having people just pour into me. So many people in my life loved me and walked with me in that dark season.

One of my coworkers suggested that I listen to the Christian radio station while I drove around for work to see if it helped my broken heart. Slowly it did. I didn't realize it at the time, but God was reaching me through song to let me feel His love.

You see, I was angry with God most days and, in my grief, just completely on autopilot. But I began to know the songs and sing them in my head even when I wasn't driving. God was placing His Word in my heart, and I was able to recall it when the pain was heavy. At the time, though, I didn't know God was at work. I only knew that I felt lighter listening to the Christian music, and I enjoyed the new connection I had with the coworker who had suggested it.

***

Years later I was sitting in a circle with my husband. We had just joined our first community group from church. When one of the younger members referred to a certain verse, I immediately had a song in my head. I mentioned it to the group, so we looked up the verse and read the passage.

"That's neat!" I said. "It's just like the verse of that song," and I sang the chorus.

With a smile she said, "Yes, most Christian music is taken from the Bible and its stories."

At that moment the light bulb went on, and I finally understood! All the years I had been listening to the music, God was filling me with His promises, with His Word. I had never read the Bible for myself outside of small-group Bible studies. I knew I felt nudges from God to read His Word, but I always had an excuse. Now I realized that, since I wouldn't read, He had spoken to me through song! I was in awe. How could the God of the universe care that much about me? Why would He want me to read His Word—and why would He want me to know Him better?

***

I am so thankful for that first community group.

A handful of married couples and a handful of college students, we were an unlikely crew. We married folks all felt old and out of touch with our cool side when we first met the younger college kids! Yet those college kids showed me such resilience and reminded me how quickly the years go by. I was growing so much with this group.

While we were in that group, I lost my job— the new job I'd been so excited about—and I was devastated. Worse than the loss of income was the fact I wasn't at all sure where to find my worth now that I wasn't employed and able to work hard at climbing *the corporate ladder. Telling this group that the company had decided to furlough my position was so embarrassing. Yet everyone in the group showed me love and grace, and week after week of my job search, they reminded me I wasn't alone.*

At the same time, my marriage was strained, and the rest of the group could see it. One week my husband, Michael, and I weren't able to fake it, and we let the group know how bad things were for us. Again, it was embarrassing. Again, the group showed us love and grace. I clearly remember sitting with the group in that living room. As we cried, one of the men stood up and reminded us of all the seasons Michael and I had made it through—together. Especially the dark season when we lost David.

Our little boy's death had come up a lot in our small group. We had shared many times about God's provision and love as we walked through our heartache. My brother-in-law and my sister-in-law mentioned David's name often, and their doing so ministered to us. It was good to know that David would never be forgotten. My brother-in-law and my sister-in-law knew well the pain and darkness we had experienced. They reminded us that Michael and I are together for a reason and that God could carry us through this tough season too. It meant a lot to Michael that his brother stood up and spoke over us.

Having that connection with our group carried us through a tough season of job loss, marriage struggles, new jobs, and growing kids. The young women I met in that group grew to be friends, and they continue to be a part of my life. We stay in touch, and I hope the joy of the Lord is obvious in our friendship.

***

It has been 10 years since David died, and Michael and I continue to live with grief. On some days the pain is raw. On other days I feel like what happened is a story I know, but I'm disconnected from the hurt. Over those 10 years I met with many counselors and had many friends who gave me permission to journey through my grief at my pace.

One thing I have discovered is, there's no way around grief. We have to walk through it. We don't have to walk through it alone, though. After I lost my job and wasn't finding work, a woman from church reached out to me. She gave me two books for Christmas and insisted that the gift need not be reciprocated. When she saw them, she explained, she thought they would be helpful for me. I was so grateful for this gift. On top of everything else, I was so lonely, and I had prayed for a friend. Her thoughtfulness really helped us become good friends.

***

I had been feeling the nudge from God to read the Bible. I sensed Him saying, "What's your excuse now, Sarah? You're not working, your kids are sleeping through the night, and they go to school during the day. You have a Book to start reading. What's your excuse now?"

One morning I got up early, and I started reading one of the books my friend had given me. The topic was waiting on God and trusting Him. In certain sections I had to open my Bible and read a passage to understand the author's point—and I realized I was doing my very own Bible study! I had never done a Bible study on my own. Now, every morning I woke up and did another chapter, and before I knew it, I had finished the book. I shared with my friend how this new morning routine was changing me and how grateful I was that God put us together to be friends.

I kept up this morning routine. Doing studies and having this daily time with God changed me. This quiet time for reflection helped me recognize all the ways God was working in my life. I was so thankful that—even though grief was hitting me hard, my marriage was struggling, and I was lonely—I was unemployed. It seemed so upside down. I was, though, so glad to have time to invest in knowing God better.

I had known God for years, but not like this. Not in such a personal way. When I was saved at 17 years old, I knew my soul was secure. I wasn't yet walking with Him all the way, though. But my coworker suggesting Christian music to heal my broken heart, the small community group showing me God was speaking to me through that music, a new friend taking a chance and reaching out to me—God used all this to show me what had been waiting for me all along. And what I had been waiting for, searching for, but didn't know I already had was an identity: my identity is in Christ alone.

***

My identity is in Christ alone—I didn't know that truth immediately. It took me many years and many friendships before I could see and believe that life-changing fact. Yes, I was a wife, a mother, a coworker, a friend, a daughter. And in every one of those identities, I strove to make sure those people I was in relationship with knew I was the best [fill in the blank: wife, mother, coworker, friend, daughter]. Everything had to be stripped away before I could finally see that God loved me... just because He loves me. Not because of anything I've done, and there's nothing I could do to earn His acceptance or more of His love.

Then, when I read Isaiah during a Lent study, I found a verse that changed me forever:

> *Thus says the LORD,*
> *he who created you, O Jacob,*
> *he who formed you, O Israel:*
> *Do not fear, for I have redeemed you;*
> *I have called you by name, you are mine."*
> *Isaiah 43:1*

Reading those words, I finally realized how much God loved me. When I finally saw that verse, my heart began to heal.

First, I allowed God to heal the hurt I had carried in my heart since losing David. I had a great counselor who taught me coping skills, and I began to see why coping skills were so important in this journey. The things she taught me were even more valuable years later when I started living in the truth that my identity is in Christ alone.

Also, my morning quiet time slowly became a time for me to read God's Word. The Bible is alive and active, breathing life into the reader and helping us understand our Creator, helping us understand that He loves us. That truth is so simple yet so complex. Until I realized and accepted this love, though, I couldn't really love others the way God intends me to love them—and He has given me some wonderful people to love. I am so thankful for the people I have met along the way in this life journey. I can look back and see the fingerprints of God on every relationship.

***

When I think about the relationships God has blessed me with and consider how important each one is, I see where God was and is in all of them. I also see that we are never walking alone because God Himself is always with us. He created us to be in community and in relationships, and He brings people into our lives to help us in different seasons. Some of those relationships endure, and others last only for a short while. I welcome all of them. Some of the most impactful people I've known are not in my everyday life, but I am thankful I received their love if only for a season. The ones who were not afraid to invest in me have changed me.

These people also helped me to walk in my identity as a child of God—walk in surrender to the One who calls me "Mine"—and to live in a way that bears fruit for the Lord. Oh, I still strive, but I'm aware when I do. I can see when I start to strive in a relationship or when I'm working on a task. When I recognize this in myself, I can pull back, stop trying to control the situation, and get back to leaning on God.

And leaning on God can happen 24/7 because I know that my God is always with me, I don't have to be afraid to be real and vulnerable with the people whom God wants me to invest in. And I hope the Holy Spirit will continue to work through me to show others, first, that their worth and their identity are in Christ alone and, second, to encourage them to walk through life in community. May they learn what I've learned, that better than hiding is reaching out and saying, "Life is hard." There's nothing like hearing a godly friend say, "Yes, life is hard, but don't lose hope. There is hope in Jesus. He loves you, and He is always with you no matter how deep the valley or dark the night."

Dear one, Sarah's story so beautifully illustrates the significance of having a community of people to support us as we journey through life. It is important—it is critical to life itself—that we don't isolate ourselves when we're struggling. Yet too often we do exactly that. Many women have told me that they feel so alone, that no one understands, and that they're ashamed of their suffering. After all— the myth goes—if you're a Christian, you shouldn't be struggling, right? Wrong. Very wrong. Jesus Christ Himself suffered when He walked on this earth, so He understands our suffering. And He, too, was part of an imperfect community, which is exactly the kind of community we, too, will always be part of. Jesus Himself experienced the truth that a community is comprised of flawed individuals who will not always be available to meet our needs.

There Is No Perfect Community

Read the following passage from Matthew 26 with me. We can learn much about our imperfect community when we look to our Lord's suffering on earth:

> Then Jesus went with [His eleven disciples] to a place called Gethsemane; and he said to his disciples, "Sit here while I go over there and pray." He took with him Peter and the two sons of Zebedee [James and John], and began to be grieved and agitated. Then he said to them, "I am deeply grieved, even to death; remain here, and stay awake with me."
>
> And going a little farther, he threw himself on the ground and prayed, "My Father, if it is possible, let this cup pass from me; yet not what I want but what you want."
>
> Then he came to the disciples and found them sleeping; and he said to Peter, "So, could you not stay awake with me one hour? Stay awake and pray that

you may not come into the time of trial; the spirit indeed is willing, but the flesh is weak."

Again he went away for the second time and prayed, "My Father, if this cannot pass unless I drink it, your will be done." Again he came and found them sleeping, for their eyes were heavy. So leaving them again, he went away and prayed for the third time, saying the same words.

Then he came to the disciples and said to them, "Are you still sleeping and taking your rest? See, the hour is at hand, and the Son of Man is betrayed into the hands of sinners. Get up, let us be going. See, my betrayer is at hand."

After Jesus had His last supper with His disciples and before He was betrayed by His disciple Judas Iscariot, Jesus spent time with His Father. There, in the garden called Gethsemane, He poured out His heart before His Father. Scripture tells us that Jesus was "deeply grieved, even to death," and Dr. Luke, in his gospel account, tells us that in Jesus' anguish, He prayed so earnestly that His sweat was like great drops of blood (Luke 22:44).

I'm sure the disciples could easily see that Jesus was upset. Why else would He have asked them—three times—to pray for Him? Yet Jesus' disciples—His tightest community for three years—couldn't be there for Jesus in His hour of greatest need. Isn't that also the time when we need our friends to pray with us and for us? Have you ever needed a friend but no one was available or willing to pray out loud for you? And what about those times when a friend needed you and you couldn't be there for her right then? I've experienced both sides of this painful situation.

Returning to the Matthew 26 passage, we learn these lessons, among others:

1. **At times people in our community can't be or won't be there for us.** Peter, James, and John could not stay awake. The gospel of Luke tells us the disciples were sleeping because of grief (Luke

⤳ TINA C. ELACQUA, PH.D. ⤳

22:45). Whatever the reason, these dear friends of Jesus did not pray with Him when He needed them to. Precious one, our friends will let us down. But God does not, and He never will.

2. **God is always available to meet with us.** That night in the garden of Gethsemane, God was awake for Jesus, and God will always be awake for us. God will never be too tired or too busy to meet with us. Still, many of us will go through our list of friends, calling one after another to find help processing our thoughts and feelings about a given situation. Rather than call our friends, let's first spend time with God. Then, if God nudges us to call Sally or Rita, we'll call her. Before you process an experience with a friend, spend time processing with the Lord Almighty.

3. **God wants you to invite His will to be done in your life.** In the garden, Jesus begged His Father to let the plan be different. Jesus knew He would be crucified, and He asked God for a different way to accomplish the forgiveness of mankind's sin. Yet after pouring out His heart to God, Jesus surrendered to the Almighty: "Your will be done." Recognizing that God the Father knows best, Jesus yielded Himself to the cross. That was, after all, God's plan.

Beloved, Jesus knew community, a very imperfect, very human community. His disciples didn't rally for Him when He most needed them. You are not alone in being disappointed by people. Still, whether we are in a time of joy or suffering, God calls us to be in community with one another. And even though no community will be perfect, God calls us—whom He created in His image—to be a part of one. After all, God Himself is a relational God.

Our Relational God Seeks Community with You and Me

The truth that God is relational is evident in His existence as a Triune God: He is One God who exists as three distinct Persons—Father,

Son, and Holy Spirit. Each of these Persons has a relationship with the other two, and each Person of God wants to be in a relationship with us.

In Genesis 2:18, the Lord said, "It is not good that the man should be alone; I will make him a helper as his partner." God designed humans to be in community with one another to help and to be helped; to support and to be supported; and to uplift and to be uplifted by one another. Likewise, when God walked with Adam and Eve, He modeled for us that He desires to be in relationship with us. Even though Adam and Eve—and each one of us after them—chose independence from God rather than relationship with Him, God continues to pursue us. He even provided the costly means for us to be in relationship with Him when He sent His only Son, Jesus Christ, to die on the cross as payment for our sins. John 3:16 tells us the Father sent His Son for our salvation, and Jesus affirmed this when He walked on earth: "I am the way, and the truth, and the life. No one comes to the Father except through me" (John 14:6).

As we look at Jesus' time on this earth, we see Him in relationship with people. Jesus had community with many people, but especially with His twelve disciples and, among those, He was closest to Peter, James, and John. Jesus immersed Himself in community and calls us to do the same. God designed us as social beings.

After Jesus' death, burial, and resurrection, He spent 40 days on earth, and on one occasion He appeared to more than 500 people (Acts 1:3; 1 Corinthians 15:6). Right before Jesus ascended to heaven, Jesus told His disciples and other believers to not leave Jerusalem—to not yet go out to fulfill the Great Commission—but to wait there for the "promise of the Father" (Acts 1:4). That promise was the Holy Spirit, the Person of God who lives within believers to guide, teach, comfort, and do so much more for us. While Jesus was on earth, He could only be in one place at a time. Since Pentecost and still today, His Spirit—the Holy Spirit—indwells all believers, enabling Jesus' love to extend all over the world (Colossians 1:27; Galatians 2:20). And Jesus' love is key to our being in community with fellow believers.

Sarah's reaching out and becoming part of a community meant that she would—according to her heavenly Father's plan—receive healing from Jesus through the believers who were part of that healthy God-centered community. And, yes, just as healthy churches display certain qualities, the fellow believers, friends, support groups, and professional counselors that comprise a healthy support community also have certain traits in common. Let's explore some of those.

A Healthy Community of Friends

When we turn to the Bible, we find characteristics to look for in a person who might become part of our support network.

1. A healthy friend turns your eyes to Jesus in the good times as well as the bad times of life. Also, with humility and gentleness, a true friend loves you enough to point out sin in your life. Remember, God's purpose is always redemption, and He will use friends to help us be free from sin (Matthew 18:15-17; Hebrews 3:12-13). When you deviate from Jesus' narrow path, a true friend—acting with wisdom, compassion, understanding, and tenderness—helps you find your way back to that narrow path. This friend has your best interest at heart and desires for you to live a righteous life. This friend knows that accepting Jesus as Savior is the only way you can be right with God and that living with Him as Lord is the only way you can live with joy in God.

> Better is open rebuke
> than hidden love.
> Well meant are the wounds a friend inflicts,
> but profuse are the kisses of an enemy.
> – Proverbs 27:5-6

> If we walk in the light as he himself is in the light,
> we have fellowship with one another, and the blood
> of Jesus his Son cleanses us from all sin. – 1 John 1:7

Iron sharpens iron,
>and one person sharpens the wits of another. –
Proverbs 27:17

Whoever walks with the wise becomes wise,
>but the companion of fools suffers harm. –
Proverbs 13:20

2. A healthy friend is always committed to you. A true friend does not walk away when you are suffering and hurting, but is instead consistently supportive and loyal whatever life brings you. This reliable friend will stay the course listening to you, encouraging you, speaking God's truth, and praying for you. This trustworthy friend will not do anything to betray your confidence. She will not gossip: your conversations will remain between the two of you.

A friend loves at all times,
>and kinsfolk are born to share adversity. –
Proverbs 17:17

Some friends play at friendship
>but a true friend sticks closer than one's nearest
kin. – Proverbs 18:24

Do not forsake your friend or the friend of your parent;
>do not go to the house of your kindred in the day
of your calamity.
Better is a neighbor who is nearby
>than kindred who are far away. – Proverbs 27:10

A perverse person spreads strife,
>and a whisperer separates close friends.
– Proverbs 16:28

3. A healthy friend is willing to go deep. Remember how Sarah's friend Stephanie asked questions and gave Sarah opportunities to talk about David? Stephanie was willing to go into the deep sorrow her friend felt and sit in the ashes with her. So she intentionally asked thought-provoking questions that would enable her to come alongside Sarah in her pain and pour into her life the healing love of Jesus. Rather than settling for a shallow relationship, a true friend wants a deep intimate relationship where both parties are genuine, transparent, and vulnerable.

> Let love be genuine; hate what is evil, hold fast to what is good; love one another with mutual affection; outdo one another in showing honor. – Romans 12:9-10

> Rejoice in hope, be patient in suffering, persevere in prayer. – Romans 12:12

> Rejoice with those who rejoice, weep with those who weep. – Romans 12:15

4. A healthy friend loves you with the love of Christ, and that kind of love is unconditional. This friend will inspire you and motivate you to love others in the selfless way that Christ loves the church. This friend will put your needs above her own needs. Jesus Christ is the ultimate example of such sacrificial love.

> "No one has greater love than this, to lay down one's life for one's friends." – John 15:13

> Do nothing from selfish ambition or conceit, but in humility regard others as better than yourselves. – Philippians 2:3

> Do not be deceived: "Bad company ruins good morals." – 1 Corinthians 15:33

5. A healthy friend helps you carry your burden of pain, sin, shame, whatever it is. A true friend is reliable. She will pray for you when she says she will. She sends you that encouraging note in the mail, takes you to lunch, and prays out loud over you. And those are just a few of the possible ways this friend who loves God and loves you can help you carry your heavy burden.

A dear friend of mine knew that the holidays would be particularly hard for me right after my parents died. So she was intentional about helping to ease my sorrow. She lived far away, but by mailing me care packages for those particularly difficult days—by relying on help from the United States Postal Service—this dear friend showed me in tangible ways that she was with me. She truly helped me to hang on to the Lord through that challenging season.

> Two are better than one… For if they fall, one will lift
> up the other; but woe to one who is alone and falls and
> does not have another to help. – Ecclesiastes 4:9-10

> Bear one another's burdens, and in this way you will
> fulfill the law of Christ. – Galatians 6:2

We can look at many more Scriptures and several more qualities of a healthy God-centered community. But even this sample points out how important our friendships with women who love Jesus are to our healing, spiritual growth, and the freedom that results.

One more thing. Don't be surprised—and definitely don't arrange—to be in a community of women who look just like you. Through the years, I have benefited greatly from women who were older than me and younger than me. Women who had a different background, nationality, and Christian testimony. But all of these women loved the Lord and desired to become more intimate with Him.

You truly will miss out on the blessings God has for you if you don't have true friends who can inspire you to look more like Jesus and to live more committed to Him. These true friends enrich our lives and enable us to walk in the liberty that Jesus' love gives.

Professional Counseling and Support Groups

Sometimes our Christ-centered friends are members of formally established support groups we are part of. I have joined several such support groups throughout my life. When I lost my parents, for instance, I became a part of a homicide support group. The special friends I met in that group helped me heal from that trauma.

Here, my dear friend Emily shares how support groups and professional counseling were foundational in enabling her to live in freedom today.

> *Failure. Divorce. Both words have seven letters, and for me, they were synonymous: marriage was yet another thing that I could not do correctly.*
>
> *Searing pain. In the brain the pain centers that register physical pain also register emotional pain. Divorce really, literally, physically hurts. It feels like death. No person dies. Just your relationship, your hopes and dreams for the future, the life you now never have. All of that is dead, and part of you died with it. The part of you that felt loved, cherished, and valued. Now you are left with raging insecurity, shame, and guilt—and the sense that you will never be able to breathe again. I kept asking myself, "Why doesn't he love me anymore? Why am I not enough? Why won't he fight for me, for our relationship? Why does this seem so easy for him and like the end of the world to me?" I remember wishing that the earth would open and swallow me whole.*
>
> *Things were so good at first. I knew that this man was God's gift for me. The relationship felt so easy. Then it was like a slow leak from a faucet. Or like small cracks in the foundation of a house. I started to see a counselor because I knew I was drowning. I also started on an antidepressant medication. I had access to all*

kinds of medications. This would become a problem for me….

I was finding it harder and harder to get out of bed, to see any hope for the future. I had tried so many different psychiatric medications, and none of them were really helping. So I started to take more and more pills. I had become suicidal. I spent more and more time thinking about swallowing the many bottles of pills I had access to.

I finally told my counselor how bad my depression had become. She and I agreed that I needed some inpatient treatment. I lasted two months before I required hospitalization again.

I knew my marriage was over, and at that point, I wished my life were over as well. Between the depression and the coming divorce, I was empty. I had absolutely nothing left. I had to take a medical leave of absence from my job, and I entered a partial hospitalization program that my insurance was refusing to cover. My employer decided to give me paid medical leave. They didn't have to do so, but they did. I didn't realize it at the time, but this generous provision was the beginning of my road back and the first of many tangible signs of His love and grace that God gave me. For a period of six weeks, I went to the hospital from 8:00-5:00, Monday through Saturday.

My job, I realized, was to focus on healing. At first, this was incredibly difficult because I didn't believe I deserved help or healing. Furthermore, with my heart shattered into a million pieces, I didn't think I would ever recover. Not enough glue or duct tape existed! But I saw that God had begun His good work; I finally realized that "My grace is sufficient for you, for my power is made perfect in weakness" (2 Corinthians 12:9, NIV). God had definitely met me in my weakness and started the process of healing me. His healing wasn't instantaneous; it has been a process with a lot of bumps and bruises along the way.

As part of the process, the Lord used the hospitalization program, its staff, and my fellow patients to show me His love. My church family also loved me well through all the pain. I continued to see my counselor for another year, and once a week I went to a support group at the hospital. Both individual therapy and group therapy were instrumental in my recovery. My mind began to clear. I had been in a fog of pain for so long. In my heart, a spark of life had been fanned into flame. I began to trust the truth of Isaiah 42:3—"A bruised reed he will not break, and a smoldering wick he will not snuff out" (NIV). The world and the enemy had tried to do both, but God had other plans for my life. I began to feel His love in new ways. He had by no means abandoned me. He loved me fiercely despite my shortcomings…He loved me despite the fact that I was depressed and hospitalized, despite the fact that my marriage had fallen apart, despite the fact that I had to take medical leave from my job, basically despite the fact that it felt like I had failed miserably at life. Yet God loved me anyway, He loved me because… Well, He just loved me—and then He restored me to my job. He deepened friendships, and He gave me a support network that helped carry me through.

All these means of support were important because I wasn't only recovering from depression; I also had to recover from the divorce. I attended the divorce hearing alone with my attorney. I cried through the whole ten minutes it took to finalize the divorce. The irony was not lost on me. The marriage began with two people, and the divorce ended with one. My life as a single person had begun.

Being divorced in a world where most people are married definitely has its challenges. The enemy loves to tell me that no one loves me, that no one will ever love me. I have learned, though, that Jesus is actually enough for me. Those words aren't just something that Christians say. Jesus really was and really is enough. He has proven Himself to me time and time again.

Jesus has also helped me recognize that I have been given the gift of singleness, the gift of being able to devote myself wholly to Him. Coming to see singleness as a gift took some time. At first, feelings of loneliness, guilt, and shame were overpowering. I wanted what everybody else had, and I saw my life as lacking. But over time God showed me that looking at my life in that way was not helpful or true. The Holy Spirit continually challenged me: "Do you really believe you can trust God, that He loves you enough to send His one and only Son to die for you?" If so, then I needed to trust this part of my life to Him as well. I needed to find my sufficiency in Him.

And this is the journey I've been on now for more than 15 years. I did not remarry. I have no children. So the world sees a poor, pitiful, middle-aged woman who will probably die alone. Praise God! I don't see myself that way anymore! I now live in the truth that I am a daughter of the King, loved perfectly by the Savior. I need no one and nothing else besides Jesus. I have found that these verses are the song of my heart:

Whom have I in heaven but you?
*   And earth has nothing I desire besides you.*
My flesh and my heart may fail,
*   but God is the strength of my heart and my portion forever.*

— Psalm 73:25-26 (NIV)

So often in Scripture, the words that follow "but God…" are precious promises. That is where I live my life now. In the time that comes after "but God…".

If part of this story sounded a little familiar to you, it's because you read some of Emily's story back in chapter 2 when she (courageously) wrote about revealing her secrets and inviting the Lord to shine His light into her darkness. Emily shared more of her story here in order to emphasize that the professional counseling she received—both individual sessions and group therapy—was instrumental in allowing her to walk in freedom. God used these very tools of therapy to bless Emily with transformational healing.

Wise Counsel

Dear one, to experience the same type of life-change Emily has known, we must choose our counselors carefully. We must be wise about whom we allow to offer us direction for our life. We discussed the importance of only opening our heart to trusted sisters in the Lord. Similarly, it is crucial for us to only let people invest in us whom the Lord has made godly and wise. As these three Scriptures reveal, God is our ultimate Counselor:

> For a child has been born for us,
>   a son given to us;
> authority rests upon his shoulders;
>   and he is named
> Wonderful Counselor, Mighty God,
>   Everlasting Father, Prince of Peace. – Isaiah 9:6

> When I look there is no one;
>   among these there is no counselor who,
>   when I ask, gives an answer. – Isaiah 41:28

> For who has known the mind of the Lord?
> Or who has been his counselor? – Romans 11:34

Yes, our heavenly Father is a wonderful and marvelous Counselor to whom none can compare; no one is His equal. This fact should guide our choice of counselors. We are to find a counselor who does the following:

1. Seeks God to counsel us through His Word. The Bible offers the blueprint for what we should think and how we should act. A counselor relying on God's guidance will be speaking God's life-changing truth into our life.

2. Follows Jesus Christ and lets his/her Christian faith inform his/her way of life. Why should we choose a *Christian* counselor? First of all, opening your mind and heart to someone who doesn't share your faith in Jesus—a faith that serves as the foundation of your life, that gives your life meaning, and that establishes your priorities and guides your behaviors—would not bring you to the healing and freedom only Jesus can give.

Also, our purpose in life is to glorify God, and one way we do so is to yield to His transformational power that makes us more and more like Christ (Romans 8:29). Furthermore, only when a counselor has a relationship with Christ can he/she have the mind of Christ (1 Corinthians 2:16).

A counselor's Christian faith, however, doesn't guarantee that the two of you will be able to work together well. Give the counselor a few sessions before deciding if he/she is right for you. Ask the Lord to give you wisdom for this decision. And don't choose a counselor simply because he/she will agree with whatever you say. Only if a counselor has the expertise and courage to help you allow the Holy Spirit to change you into the person God created you to be—a person who can live in freedom—will your efforts in counseling be worthwhile.

3. Offers expertise based on specific training for the specific issues we are dealing with. For example, when I suffered the trauma of my parents' murder, I searched for a counselor who specialized in trauma. I also joined a group of folks who experienced loss of loved ones in a variety of ways. It was helpful, but not to the same degree as the support group I joined that was comprised of individuals who had lost a loved one to homicide.

Beloved, I hope these testimonies have not only inspired you but have also reinforced the importance of not isolating yourself. The life-giving support of a Christian community is wonderful in times of joy and absolutely critical in times of sorrow. The truth is, God has wired you for relationships. He created you to be in relationship with Him and with people. He wants you to be in fellowship with others not only to receive but also to give—to love them, encourage them, speak truth to them, help them carry their burden, and celebrate with them the Lord's answers to their prayers. And, dear one, our relational God also seeks to have one-on-one time with you each day. He will always be available to listen, to speak to you, to comfort you, and He longs to prepare your heart to recognize His will—His best for you—and obey. God wants you to abide in Him, walk in relationship with Him, and be His hands and feet to those in need.

PERSONAL REFLECTION AND APPLICATION

1. Are you part of a church community? A small-group community? A group-therapy community? If so, what are a couple benefits or blessings you've experienced?

If you're not in community, will you begin seeking community? Why/why not? Think about what you learned in this chapter and what Sarah's story teaches about the value of community.

2. Think about and list below a few friends you live life with. Who can you lean on when you're struggling? Who do you laugh with? Who do you know will pray for you? Which friend(s) can you study God's Word with? And which friend(s) point you to the Father?

If no one comes to mind, know you are not alone in that. In today's culture of social media, many individuals find themselves alone and without anyone they would call a close friend. Many others of us strain to find a kindred spirit or two. So spend time now asking the Lord to bring into your life—into your inner circle—people who have the qualities of a healthy friend.

If you are able to name three to five friends you can call on in times of joy and sorrow, evaluate your friendships according the five key qualities for a healthy friend described in this chapter:

- In what ways does your friend turn your eyes to Jesus?
- Are you able to say your friend is always committed to you? Why or why not?
- Is your friend willing to go deep in a relationship and, for instance, enter your pain? Give an example.
- Does your friend love you with the love of Christ? If so, please give a couple examples.
- What does your friend do to help you carry your burden of pain, sin, shame, whatever it is?

Now ask yourself these same questions:

- In what ways do you turn your friends' eyes to Jesus?
- Are you truly committed to your friends? Why or why not?
- Are you willing to go deep in a relationship and, for instance, enter your friend's pain? Give an example or two of a time you have journeyed with a friend through a painful experience.
- Do you love your friends with the love of Christ? If so, please give a couple examples.
- What do you do to help your friends carry their burden of pain, sin, shame, or whatever else it is?

If you realize that you aren't as good a friend as you thought you were, what are some specific changes you can make to be a better friend? Think about anyone you know who seems to breathe life into people, especially people who are hurting, lonely, or burdened by sin and shame. What can you learn from the example of individuals who are able to love with God's warm, accepting, and sacrificial love? What supportive behaviors can you do for people you care about?

3. Are you stuck? Do you think the Lord may be leading you to receive professional counseling in order to move forward toward a life of freedom? Perhaps, as Emily shared, individual and/or group therapy would help you process your pain at a deeper level than can realistically be done in a community of trusted sisters in Christ. If so, spend some time now asking the Lord to direct you to the wise counsel that would be of great benefit.

PRAYER: Heavenly Father, Jesus, my Lord and Savior, and Holy Spirit, You are a relational God who designed me to be in relationship with others—to be in community with others—who can love me, encourage me, and hold me accountable to becoming more and more like Jesus. You alone are my Healer, yet You may choose to use people I am in community with or professional counselors to help heal my pain and sorrow. Take these broken pieces of my life, I ask, and use the people whom You deem appropriate for this miraculous work of restoration to wholeness. Heal me in such a way that I can live in freedom.

CHAPTER **EIGHT**

Sharing Your Story

JEN SHARES HER STORY below…

I was a sophomore in high school. She and I had become friends, good friends. Until the relationship became more than friends.

She was staying the night at my house, I was falling asleep next to her, and that was when we first kissed. I remember wondering, "Is this how it should be? Is this wrong?"

I was confused and paralyzed. I didn't say anything, and she never said anything. Instead of talking, we let it just progress. Soon, rather than feeling confused, I just began to feel the pleasure of it—until it was over. Then I felt the shame of it. But I had so separated my life of sin from my life of light, that in the daytime I actually forgot about it. It was as if my life of sin was only for the night, only for the darkness, and during the day and in the light, it didn't exist.

***

One time my dad thought he saw us kiss. That was definitely what he saw, but when my mom confronted me, I lied to her. I was practiced in lying because I had already been lying to myself and, ultimately, to God. There is something about sin that feeds other sins. When we have obscured and hidden the truth, we seem to forget how to speak it. Even though my mom's confrontation was kind, I couldn't tell her the truth.

As I sat in the quiet of her room, she asked if my relationship with my friend was pure, and she encouraged me to be careful. I listened as she said things I already knew to be true: our bodies are temples of the Holy Spirit, and it is a quiet tiptoe from temptation into sin. Even though I lied to her gentle prodding for truth, my mom planted a seed of knowing in my heart. I had heard her love for me as she spoke the truth, and I began to understand that what I was doing was not actually what I wanted to be doing. I began to realize and know in my heart that I was not free and that this pleasure was not—and never would be—satisfying.

I began to pray. I wasn't praying for the relationship to end or for the courage of the Lord to help me end it. I just began to pray that the Lord would cleanse me and lead me. I know my mom was praying for me as well. She didn't ask again about my friend and me, but from time to time she would remind me of the truth that purity and holiness are important to God. She would also remind me that I am a vessel and that the Lord wants to use me in this world. I don't think it was too much time after she spoke to me and I began to pray that I knew what I had to do.

***

One morning, I turned away from the desire for another woman's body, and I looked up. With courage I believe can only come from the Spirit, I told my friend that I was a hypocrite. "I can't do this anymore," I said to her.

She was upset. I knew she would be. I had not been good to her; I had not been genuine or honest with her or myself, with the Lord or my family. I apologized to my friend and asked for her forgiveness. My friend did forgive me and remained—remains—my friend. And even though I had blurred the lines between light and dark, the Lord's love for me had remained.

In one moment I knew what freedom was. I was released. In the Spirit of the Lord, I found the courage to see my sin for what it was. To see my hypocrisy, the malice, and the ugliness that had come from the misuse of my body for unsatisfying and temporary pleasure. My God-fearing mother had planted a seed, and I experienced in my heart an ever-growing desire to be used by God to bring other people to His love. The seed had grown because of prayer, and it had blossomed because of the encouragement of fellow believers. You see, I'd remained in the body of the believers—in the church—while I lived in my sin. The consistent presence of God's people in my life and the way their examples challenged me to go deeper in my walk with the Lord watered and nourished the seed my mother had sown.

However, my journey was not yet over.

∗∗∗

My journey out of the dark wasn't over because I had yet to tell the truth—and I was afraid to do so. How could I tell those people who had seen me in the light that I had also been living in the dark? How could I replace the lie I had been living with the truth about *who I was now, forgiven, healed, and free? What would the people at church say about me? What would they say to me? I had found freedom from sin, but shame was now my prison.*

At first, I told my fellow believers I was nailing lust to the cross, and that was true—as far as it went. I wasn't just nailing lust to the cross; I was nailing homosexual desire. I had been choosing flesh over spirit. I had decided—again and again—to actively use my body for pleasure outside of the boundaries Jesus has established.

For three years after I turned my head from sin and from this unsatisfying thing, I had yet to name what it was that I had been freed from. I had yet to speak the truth of my story until...

***

I hadn't truthfully shared my story with anyone until, sitting in a café with two friends, one of them shared her testimony. Betty told us of her experience with the Lord and how her life had changed in a moment. I got to thinking about my own experience of recognizing my sin, repenting, and receiving salvation, and I realized I had a story to tell. Betty's honesty gave me the courage to be honest. Her faith showed me that the Lord's grace is greater in our greatest weakness, and even though I was still afraid, I spoke. I shared my story, and my two friends in that cafe loved me despite of and in light of what I told them about myself. They didn't see me as my sin; instead, they celebrated the freedom I had found in the love of Christ Jesus.

I began to pray for the courage to tell more people my story. I wanted to share the light of Christ, a light that was much brighter than the darkness of my own desires. I began to tell close friends. One friend. Two friends. Nine friends heard my whole story from beginning to end.

A whole crowd heard it.

An adult heard it.

Fourteen more people heard it.

Arms opened to me. Hearts connected with mine. The Spirit met me through His people.

I continued to find more and more freedom, and my fear about sharing my story was becoming weaker and weaker. And now when I'm tempted, now when I'm bound by the shame, and now when I'm again afraid of what my flesh might urge me to do, people around me pray. Now when I'm worried that I'm falling again, slipping again, I find myself making a counseling appointment or getting coffee with a trusted sister in Christ. Because I've shared my story, I've found people who want to be with me—people who help me drive away the shame, who offer life in Christ to me, and who encourage me to continue walking in the narrow path of our Lord Jesus Christ.

As you will discover, there is great value in telling your story. I would even say it is essential to the healing process. Furthermore, when we tell our story, God can use it to build up the body of Christ.

Now we'll look at how we go about telling our story, determining what we share and what we cut. In each chapter of this book, we've looked at something that is fundamental to our story. I'll explain more fully by using the story of my dear friend Jen. Hers is the story you just read.

Telling Your Story to Glorify God

Of course there isn't one prescribed format or one right way to share your story. Here, though, I offer eight ideas about how to tell your story in a way that truly gives God glory. I'll use excerpts from Jen's story as examples.

1. Come out of hiding. Jen named her secret: homosexuality. She wrote, *One morning, I turned away from the desire for another woman's body, and I looked up. With courage I believe can only come from the Spirit, I told my friend that I was a hypocrite. "I can't do this anymore," I said to her.*

2. Shine God's light into the darkness. In response to Jen's prayers, the Lord exposed the darkness in her life for what it was: *I wanted to share the light of Christ, a light that was much brighter than the darkness of my own desires.*

3. Identify the context for healing and hope. Jen realized that her struggle with sin was the very context God would use to draw her into a deeper relationship with Him. She would experience the Lord's power and be used as an instrument to turn others to Him. Jen desired God to use her and clearly stated her context (sin) for healing and hope: *In the Spirit of the Lord, I found the courage to see my sin for what it was. To see my hypocrisy, the malice, and the ugliness that had come from the misuse of my body for unsatisfying and temporary pleasure.*

4. Talk about if and how God used your biblical faith and classic spiritual disciplines to bring healing. Jen shared that God brought healing through her own biblical faith and the spiritual disciplines of prayer, Bible study, and worship, but He didn't stop there. He also used people in her church community to encourage her and be channels of His healing love: *The seed had grown because of prayer, and it had blossomed because of the encouragement of fellow believers. You see, I'd remained in the body of the believers—in the church— while I lived in my sin. The consistent presence of God's people in my life and the way their examples challenged me to go deeper in my walk with the Lord watered and nourished the seed my mother had sown.*

5. Explain the role of forgiveness in your pursuit of freedom. Jen asked her friend to forgive her, and she asked God to forgive her: *I got to thinking about my own experience of recognizing my sin, repenting, and receiving salvation, and I realized I had a story to tell.*

6. If God used the church and its resources in your quest for healing, share some specifics. Jen remained in the church body and was open to the truth spoken by her fellow believers and her Christian parents: *Even though I lied to her gentle prodding for truth, my mom planted a seed of knowing in my heart. I had heard her love for me as she spoke the truth, and I began to understand that what I was doing was not actually what I wanted to be doing. I began to realize and know in my heart that I was not free and that this pleasure was not—and never would be—satisfying.*

7. Describe the life-giving support you received from a Christian community. Jen benefited from the support of her mom, dad, friends, and a professional counselor: all were instrumental in helping her pursue holiness and remain in holiness. *I continued to find more and more freedom, and my fear about sharing my story was becoming weaker and weaker. And now when I'm tempted, now when I'm bound by the shame, and now when I'm again afraid of what my flesh might urge me to do, people around me pray. Now when I am worried that I am falling again, slipping again, I find myself making a counseling appointment or getting coffee with a trusted sister in Christ. Because I've shared my story, I have found people who want to be with me— people who help me drive away the shame, who offer life in Christ to me, and who encourage me to continue walking in the narrow path of our Lord Jesus Christ.*

8. Share your story. Hearing a friend's story helped Jen take the step of faith and share her own story: *Betty's honesty gave me the courage to be honest. Her faith showed me that the Lord's grace is greater in our greatest weakness, and even though I was still afraid, I spoke. I shared my story, and my two friends in that cafe loved me despite of and in* *light of what I told them about myself. They didn't see me as my sin; instead, they celebrated the freedom I had found in the love of Christ Jesus. I began to pray for the courage to tell more people my story. I wanted to share the light of Christ, a light that was much brighter than the darkness of my own desires.*

Be Cautious About Telling Your Story

Friends, someone has described the story each of us has to tell as our gold, and we don't share our gold with just anyone. Keep that in mind as I share some lessons I've learned about telling my story.

1. Ask the Holy Spirit to make clear whom He wants you to share your story with (Romans 8:14). Whether or not the people you tell are believers, be sure they are individuals you can trust to receive this precious part of your heart. Again, don't think you have to tell your story to everyone even if they ask. Ask the Holy Spirit to make clear who He wants you to share your story with and when.

2. When you tell your story, only share information that will help you heal (Matthew 7:6). For example, when I talk about my parents' murder, I don't give all the gory details. Dwelling on the specifics would not help me heal. Instead, those evil particulars would draw me toward, if not into, the pit of despair. Feeling hopeless is exactly where Satan wants me, but I refuse to go there. I refuse to think too much about the horrors done to my parents. And I encourage you, precious one, to refuse Satan's request or the friends who appear interested, but who are just curious about the sensational drama.

3. Guard the heart of your audience (Proverbs 4:23). I have a friend who is quite comfortable telling her story, but she tends to share too much information which leaves many people feeling uncomfortable. Her listeners are usually not trained professionals who can handle hearing heart-wrenching details of her trauma. So instead of leaving the audience inspired to get to know God better or awed by His work in her life, they feel unsettled and find themselves wrestling with many questions. The details might even have served as triggers for their own dreadful circumstances. We never want to inadvertently nudge a listener into a downward spiral of destruction, despair, and hopelessness.

4. Realize that God can use your story to encourage many (Matthew 28:19). God has allowed you to live this unique story—specific to only you—for, among other reasons, to give you a tool for making disciples. God can use your experiences to introduce people to what a saving relationship with Jesus is all about. Suppose, for instance, you have aborted a child. If you're speaking to a group of women, you can be fairly certain that some in the audience also had an abortion. Know that every woman—whether or not she has had an abortion—will benefit from hearing your story and the lessons the Lord taught you through that dark time and because of it. I've facilitated my Hope Beyond Loss class many times, but I've never had in that class a fellow sister or brother in Christ whose loved one was murdered like my parents were. Yet what the Lord taught me in those dark years was still relevant to my brothers and sisters in Christ when they lost loved ones to suicide, cancer, old age, or something else. Again, each of us—and that includes you—has a unique and important story that God wants you to use to help make disciples of Christ.

5. Sharing about how the Lord met you in your darkness encourages others to share their story. (When Jen heard Betty's story, she wanted to share her own story.) During the last few weeks in a Hope Beyond Loss group, all the members share their story. We listen and then tell them which truths they learned on their journey ministered to us. Also, many members end up sharing more of their own personal story than they planned because someone in the group had the courage to share their story first.

Your Turn

Precious friend, I am proud of you for allowing the Lord to heal and transform your heart after the pain you've experienced. I encourage you to persevere in your journey toward living in freedom. And I pray that you have so desired to live in freedom that you have taken some, if not all, of these hard steps:

- Acknowledge your secrets and bring them into the light (chapter 1).
- Lay your hidden thoughts, feelings, and actions—all of the unspeakable experiences—at the cross of Jesus and invite God to shine His light into your darkness (chapter 2).
- Explore the biblical truths that God allowed these wounds to be inflicted, but that God didn't abandon you during those painful times (chapter 3).
- Accept the truth that God uses struggles—those you may have brought on yourself, those that resulted because we're all sinners, and those that come because we live in a fallen world—to mold us into the image of Jesus. God has the ability and the desire to use those wounds as the very context for your healing so you can live in freedom (chapter 3).
- Embrace biblical faith and—if you weren't already doing so—start to practice the spiritual disciplines of Bible study, prayer, and worship... and then begin building these tools into your daily rhythm of life (chapter 4).
- Allow the Holy Spirit to help you forgive—and you may need to forgive God, yourself, and the people who intentionally or unintentionally inflicted great harm (chapter 5).
- If you aren't already part of one, search for a vibrant church community led by a Bible-teaching pastor, filled with people committed to living out biblical truth, and offering resources that equip you to live out your faith and to make disciples (chapter 6).

- Take advantage of community support, develop a network of healthy friends, receive professional Christian counseling, and/or participate in support groups (chapter 7).

So now, beloved, you are ready to share your story. Follow whatever tips outlined above are helpful. You might also review your answers to the Reflection Questions at the end of each chapter. Your answers will provide details for your story.

One More Story

Before I close, I want to share one more story. What follows is actually a eulogy given by a friend for a friend who represents what this book is about: living in freedom. Just like us, Virginia experienced trials, pain, loss, and loneliness in life, but she followed a biblical road map and navigated life's pain in a manner that enabled her to draw closer to her Lord and to invest in the lives of those God placed within her sphere of influence.

> *If one thing symbolizes the life of Virginia Quincy Hatlen, it's her Bible. Her hospitality was warm and wonderful... Her homemade bread was amazing... But when I think of Virginia, I think of her Bible. Now, she had several Bibles, but the one I'm thinking of is— if I remember correctly—red leather. Well-worn red leather. That Book would lie open nicely no matter what passage she looked up. Clearly, it had not spent much time on a shelf or a coffee table.*
>
> *The best part of that precious Bible, though, was what Virginia had written in it. On whatever page she opened to...there... in the margins... were dates and a three- or maybe four-word note to herself. I never looked closely: that was Virginia's conversation with God. But I know that she noted the date when God gave*

her a certain verse for a specific situation or when God had fulfilled a promise for her.

Virginia had confidence in God's promises... because she knew the Promise-Maker. She knew Him very well.

During life's hard times, Virginia leaned on God and found Him absolutely faithful. And in those dark times, Virginia's faith grew, and so did her wisdom.

For example, Jesus said, "Blessed are those who mourn, for they will be comforted" (Matthew 5:4). And Virginia pointed out, "Being comforted is different from having all our questions answered."

She also observed that what can look like a dead end to us... is a U-turn toward better places.

Virginia would say, "Praise your way through dark times"—and she acknowledged that doing so would be a sacrifice of praise.

She encouraged us to use God's truth to rebuke the lies that we wrongly believe.

And when circumstances say one thing and God's Word says another, cling to God's Word.

But Virginia's favorite words of encouragement were words of Scripture that celebrate and proclaim God's love for us. She was always ready to say from memory truths like...

The Lord is gracious and merciful,
    slow to anger and abounding in steadfast love.
The Lord is good to all,
    and his compassion is over all that he has made
(Psalm 145:8-9).

Jesus has said, "I will never leave you nor forsake you" (Hebrews 13:5).

The Lord is my helper; I will not be afraid. What can anyone do to me?" (Hebrews 13:6).

The Lord, your God...will rejoice over you with gladness,
>*he will renew you in his love;*
>*he will exult over you with loud singing (Zephaniah 3:17).*

...Nothing in all creation will ever be able to separate us from the love of God...(Romans 8:39, NLT).

See what love the Father has given us, that we should be called children of God... (I John 3:1).

Jesus said, "I chose you" (John 15:16).

When I was going through some Bible verses Virginia had given me... and a journal I kept of the wisdom and encouragement she poured into my life... I found a gem I want to share: the BLESS Prayer*—and BLESS is an acronym... which I'll get to in a minute.

First, I want to read what Virginia said about this prayer:

[It's the] best prayer to pray for others—especially for your enemies—and for those you love—and for the irregular people in your life.

Lord, I pray for_____, and I ask that You would bless him/her.

Please BLESS his/her:
B — body with health and healing
L — labor and the fruit of his/her hands
E — emotions with love, joy, and peace
S — socially with friends and family

S — spiritually with salvation, sanctification, and the infilling of the Holy Spirit

BLESS: body.... labor... emotions... social... spiritual

But BLESS was more than what Virginia prayed. It's what she lived.

I know that each of you could—without hesitation— easily think of five ways Virginia blessed you. Here are my five:

- She made Christ's love more real to me—and to all of you, I'm sure, and to countless people outside this building.
- She believed for people who, in the darkness and pain of life, struggled to believe.
- She prayed for people who were too tired to pray.
- She hoped for people who were without hope.
- She shared the lifeline of God's Word that she knew so well and loved so much.

She warmly and freely spoke of her confidence in God and what she knew from experience about His character and His love.

Virginia would want you to know—and to rest in—the truths of Psalm 139. In fact, she'd probably encourage you to memorize all 24 verses. I'm only going to read two:

You formed my inward parts;
you knit me together in my mother's womb.
I praise you, for I am fearfully and wonderfully made.
Wonderful are your works;
my soul knows it very well.

And all of us know Virginia was indeed fearfully and wonderfully and beautifully made...

She was a woman whose faith in God was winsome and bright...

A woman whom God used to love people with His love...

We will miss her... but we have the hope of heaven, and we will see her again!

God bless you. May God bless you with an ever-growing knowledge of Him and an ever-deepening love for Him. Amen.

* Written by evangelist David Wilkerson (1953-2011)

Final Thoughts

I wrote *Living in Freedom: A Biblical Road Map for Navigating Life's Pain* to provide you, dear one, with a Bible-based and real-life practical book that will help you navigate life's struggles and arrive at a place of freedom, a place of emotional and spiritual health.

Not a single one of us is spared heartache, pain, and loss in this fallen world. And that means every one of us has a story to tell. Our hearts have been impacted by the darker chapters of our lives, impacted for better (we become, for instance, more compassionate, empathetic, and dependent on God) and impacted for worse (we hide behind masks, harden our hearts for protection, assume a victim mentality, withdraw from relationships, including our relationship with God—and the list goes on). We need biblical and practical direction on how to thrive in life despite experiences that wound and scar.

I hope I have helped you to better understand how to process and cope with pain; I hope you feel better equipped to live victoriously in Jesus Christ. The Personal Reflection and Application section at the end of each chapter allowed you to engage with the material in a life-transforming manner, within a community of fellow travelers. At the same time those sections prepared you to tell your story.

I also hope you've received a better understanding and appreciation of the struggles women experience but perhaps rarely, if ever, share. The information in these pages has armed you—whether you yourself are a survivor or the friend, mother, or sister of one—to walk through your own struggles and to minister to other hurting women by pointing them to the only hope we have in this fallen world: Jesus Christ.

As you navigate the minefields of pain and the darkness of life's greatest trials, I pray you will be anchored in God's Word and able to share your personal story. When you do, you'll bring words of comfort, healing, and hope to hurting people.

Also, as you continue to live according to the truths of this book, you will experience more fully the abundant life that comes with abiding in Christ, living according to God's Word, and walking in freedom, yielded to and led by the Holy Spirit.

As you live in freedom, you will help those around you—just as Virginia Quincy Hatlen did—to live in freedom as well.

APPENDIX:
GOD'S WORD FOR LIFE'S CHALLENGES

The verses below are only some of the truths that can be a lifeline as we journey through life.

Justice

Let justice roll down like waters,
    and righteousness like an ever-flowing stream.
~ Amos 5:24

"Will not God grant justice to his chosen ones who cry to him day and night? Will he delay long in helping them?"
~ Luke 18:7

God is a righteous judge,
    and a God who has indignation every day.
~ Psalm 7:11

At the presence of the LORD, for he is coming
    to judge the earth.
He will judge the world with righteousness,
    and the peoples with equity.
~ Psalm 98:9

The heavens declare his righteousness,
for God himself is judge.
~ Psalm 50:6

"Do not judge, and you will not be judged; do not condemn, and you will not be condemned. Forgive, and you will be forgiven."
~ Luke 6:37

A bruised reed he will not break,
and a dimly burning wick he will not quench;
he will faithfully bring forth justice.
~ Isaiah 42:3

Life After a Loss

We do not want you to be uninformed, brothers and sisters, about those who have died, so that you may not grieve as others do who have no hope. For since we believe that Jesus died and rose again, even so, through Jesus, God will bring with him those who have died. For this we declare to you by the word of the Lord, that we who are alive, who are left until the coming of the Lord, will by no means precede those who have died. For the Lord himself, with a cry of command, with the archangel's call and with the sound of God's trumpet, will descend from heaven, and the dead in Christ will rise first. Then we who are alive, who are left, will be caught up in the clouds together with them to meet the Lord in the air; and so we will be with the Lord forever. Therefore encourage one another with these words.
~ 1 Thessalonians 4:13-18

We are afflicted in every way, but not crushed; perplexed, but not driven to despair; persecuted, but not forsaken; struck down, but not destroyed.
~ 2 Corinthians 4:8-9

"Find your joy in the LORD."
~ Isaiah 58:14 (NIV)

Grace, mercy, and peace will be with us from God the Father and from Jesus Christ, the Father's Son, in truth and love.
~ 2 John 1:3

I am convinced that neither death, nor life, nor angels, nor rulers, nor things present, nor things to come, nor powers, nor height, nor depth, nor anything else in all creation, will be able to separate us from the love of God in Christ Jesus our Lord.
~ Romans 8:38-39

You who revere my name the sun of righteousness shall rise, with healing in its wings. You shall go out leaping like calves from the stall.
~ Malachi 4:2

Even though you intended to do harm to me, God intended it for good, in order to preserve a numerous people, as he is doing today.
~ Genesis 50:20

We know that in all things God works for the good of those who love him, who have been called according to his purpose.
~ Romans 8:28 (NIV)

This is God,
    our God forever and ever.
    He will be our guide forever.
~ Psalm 48:14

I shall not die, but I shall live,
    and recount the deeds of the LORD.
~ Psalm 118:17

Physical Symptoms

As for me, afflicted and in pain—
    may your salvation, God, protect me.
~ Psalm 69:29 (NIV)

"He will wipe every tear from their eyes.
Death will be no more;
mourning and crying and pain will be no more,
for the first things have passed away."
~ Revelation 21:4

His anger is but for a moment;
his favor is for a lifetime.
Weeping may linger for the night,
but joy comes with the morning.
~ Psalm 30:5

The spirit of the Lord GOD is upon me,
    because the LORD has anointed me;
he has sent me to bring good news to the oppressed,
    to bind up the brokenhearted,
to proclaim liberty to the captives,
    and release to the prisoners;
to proclaim the year of the LORD's favor,
    and the day of vengeance of our God;
    to comfort all who mourn;
to provide for those who mourn in Zion—
    to give them a garland instead of ashes,
the oil of gladness instead of mourning,
    the mantle of praise instead of a faint spirit.
They will be called oaks of righteousness,
    the planting of the LORD, to display his glory.
~ Isaiah 61:1-3

Praise be to the God and Father of our Lord Jesus Christ, the Father
of compassion and the God of all comfort, who comforts us in all
our troubles, so that we can comfort those in any trouble with the
comfort we ourselves receive from God.
~ 2 Corinthians 1:3-4 (NIV)

Feelings & Symptoms

Do not worry about anything, but in everything by prayer and supplication with thanksgiving let your requests be made known to God. And the peace of God, which surpasses all understanding, will guard your hearts and your minds in Christ Jesus.
~ Philippians 4:6-7

Cast your burden on the LORD,
    and he will sustain you;
he will never permit
    the righteous to be moved.
~ Psalm 55:22

God did not give us a spirit of cowardice, but rather a spirit of power and of love and of self-discipline.
~ 2 Timothy 1:7

"In your anger do not sin": Do not let the sun go down while you are still angry, and do not give the devil a foothold.
~ Ephesians 4:26-27 (NIV)

Rid yourselves of all such things as these: anger, rage, malice, slander, and filthy language from your lips.
~ Colossians 3:8 (NIV)

"This is why I have let you live: to show you my power, and to make my name resound through all the earth."
~ Exodus 9:16

"If the Son makes you free, you will be free indeed."
~ John 8:36

"'If you can'?" said Jesus. "Everything is possible for one who believes."
~ Mark 9:23 (NIV)

Now to him who by the power at work within us is able to accomplish abundantly far more than all we can ask or imagine, to him be glory in the church and in Christ Jesus to all generations, forever and ever. Amen.
~ Ephesians 3:20-21

Saying Goodbye

O that I might have my request,
    and that God would grant my desire.
~ Job 6:8

You will have confidence, because there is hope;
    you will be protected and take your rest in safety.
~ Job 11:18

He who rescued us from so deadly a peril will continue to rescue us; on him we have set our hope that he will rescue us again.
~ 2 Corinthians 1:10

Sleep Problems

It is in vain that you rise up early
    and go late to rest,
eating the bread of anxious toil;
    for he gives sleep to his beloved.
~ Psalm 127:2

If you sit down, you will not be afraid;
    when you lie down, your sleep will be sweet.
~ Proverbs 3:24

I will both lie down and sleep in peace;
    for you alone, O LORD, make me lie down in safety.
~ Psalm 4:8

"Come to me, all you that are weary and are carrying heavy burdens, and I will give you rest. Take my yoke upon you, and learn from me; for I am gentle and humble in heart, and you will find rest for your souls. For my yoke is easy, and my burden is light."
~ Matthew 11:28-30

Spiritual Life Issues

"I am the way, and the truth, and the life. No one comes to the Father except through me."
~ John 14:6

There is a time for everything,
and a season for every activity under the heavens:
    a time to be born and a time to die. . .
    a time to kill and a time to heal. . .
    a time to weep and a time to laugh,
    a time to mourn and a time to dance. . .
    a time for war and a time for peace.
~ Ecclesiastes 3:1-4, 8 (NIV)

My times are in your hand.
~ Psalm 31:15

My eyes are fixed on you, Sovereign LORD;
    in you I take refuge.
~ Psalm 141:8 (NIV)

No one who hopes in you
    will ever be put to shame,
but shame will come on those
    who are treacherous without cause.
~ Psalm 25:3 (NIV)

After you have suffered for a little while, the God of all grace, who has called you to his eternal glory in Christ, will himself restore, support, strengthen, and establish you.
~ 1 Peter 5:10

God has said, "Never will I leave you; never will I forsake you."
~ Hebrews 13:5 (NIV)

I consider that the sufferings of this present time are not worth comparing with the glory about to be revealed to us.
~ Romans 8:18

"You will know the truth, and the truth will make you free."
~ John 8:32

"My thoughts are not your thoughts,
    nor are your ways my ways, says the Lord.
For as the heavens are higher than the earth,
    so are my ways higher than your ways
    and my thoughts than your thoughts."
~ Isaiah 55:8-9

We walk by faith, not by sight.
~ 2 Corinthians 5:7

"Strive first for the kingdom of God and his righteousness, and all these things will be given to you as well."
~ Matthew 6:33

Support Network

"For God so loved the world that he gave his only Son, so that everyone who believes in him may not perish but may have eternal life."
~ John 3:16

"You are precious in my sight,
and honored, and I love you."
~ Isaiah 43:4

They confronted me in the day of my calamity;
but the LORD was my support.
~ Psalm 18:18

"I will not fail you or forsake you."
~ Joshua 1:5

It is not you that support the root, but the root that supports you.
~ Romans 11:18

Two are better than one, because they have a good reward for their toil. For if they fall, one will lift up the other; but woe to one who is alone and falls and does not have another to help.
~ Ecclesiastes 4:9-10

Where there is no guidance, a nation falls,
but in an abundance of counselors there is safety.
~ Proverbs 11:14

You, O Lord, do not be far away!
O my help, come quickly to my aid!
~ Psalm 22:19

When the righteous cry for help, the LORD hears,
and rescues them from all their troubles.
~ Psalm 34:17

"Call to me and I will answer you, and will tell you great and hidden things that you have not known."
~ Jeremiah 33:3

I call upon God,
    and the Lord will save me.
Evening and morning and at noon
    I utter my complaint and moan,
    and he will hear my voice.
~ Psalm 55:16-17

The Lord is near to all who call on him,
    to all who call on him in truth.
~ Psalm 145:18

The Lord is near to the brokenhearted,
    and saves the crushed in spirit.
~ Psalm 34:18

I can do all things through him who strengthens me.
~ Philippians 4:13

Jesus looked at them [his disciples] and said, "For mortals it is impossible, but for God all things are possible."
~ Matthew 19:26

God is our refuge and strength,
    a very present help in trouble.
~ Psalm 46:1

The LORD is my strength and my shield;
    in him my heart trusts;
so I am helped, and my heart exults,
    and with my song I give thanks to him.
The Lord is the strength of his people;
    he is the saving refuge of his anointed.
~ Psalm 28:7-8

The LORD is far from the wicked,
>   but he hears the prayer of the righteous.
~ Proverbs 15:29

Let your steadfast love become my comfort
>   according to your promise to your servant.
~ Psalm 119:76

Unwanted & Intrusive Thoughts

We demolish arguments and every pretension that sets itself up against the knowledge of God, and we take captive every thought to make it obedient to Christ.
~ 2 Corinthians 10:5 (NIV)

Prepare your minds for action; discipline yourselves; set all your hope on the grace that Jesus Christ will bring you when he is revealed.
~ 1 Peter 1:13

Whatever is true, whatever is honorable, whatever is just, whatever is pure, whatever is pleasing, whatever is commendable, if there is any excellence and if there is anything worthy of praise, think about these things.
~ Philippians 4:8

There is now no condemnation for those who are in Christ Jesus.
~ Romans 8:1 (NIV)

Vigilance

"Can any of you by worrying add a single hour to your span of life?"
~ Matthew 6:27 and Luke 12:25

Trust in the LORD with all your heart,
    and do not rely on your own insight.
In all your ways acknowledge him,
    and he will make straight your paths.
~ Proverbs 3:5-6

Bless those who persecute you; bless and do not curse them. Rejoice with those who rejoice, weep with those who weep. Live in harmony with one another; do not be haughty, but associate with the lowly; do not claim to be wiser than you are. Do not repay anyone evil for evil, but take thought for what is noble in the sight of all. If it is possible, so far as it depends on you, live peaceably with all. Beloved, never avenge yourselves, but leave room for the wrath of God; for it is written, "Vengeance is mine, I will repay, says the Lord." No, "if your enemies are hungry, feed them; if they are thirsty, give them something to drink; for by doing this you will heap burning coals on their heads." Do not be overcome by evil, but overcome evil with good.
~ Romans 12:14-21

Be strong and courageous. Do not be afraid or terrified because of them, for the Lord your God goes with you; he will never leave you nor forsake you.
~ Deuteronomy 31:6 (NIV)

The Lord himself goes before you and will be with you; he will never leave you nor forsake you. Do not be afraid; do not be discouraged.
~ Deuteronomy 31:8 (NIV)

You rejoice, even if now for a little while you have had to suffer various trials, so that the genuineness of your faith—being more precious than gold that, though perishable, is tested by fire—may be found to result in praise and glory and honor when Jesus Christ is revealed.
~ 1 Peter 1:6-7

THANK YOU

As I mentioned at the beginning of the book, being still before the Lord and meditating on His Word has been integral to my healing and my ability to live each day in freedom. That's why—and I hope this will be a blessing to you—I created a PDF file of "God's Word for Life's Challenges." The list of scriptures chosen for each life challenge I address is suitable for framing.

To download your free "God's Word for Life's Challenges," please enter this address into your web browser.

http://doralcove.com/gods-word-for-lifes-challenges/

Please don't forget to download your free bonus gift. Also, will you please help me by leaving a review for *Living in Freedom: A Biblical Road Map for Navigating Life's Pain* on Amazon?

Please enter this address into your web browser to leave a review for the book.

https://amazon.com/author/drtelacqua

LEARN MORE ABOUT
TINA, VICKI, AND LISA

Dr. Tina Elacqua is the founder and president of Doral Cove Ministries. A personal survivor of tragedy, she is passionate about bringing comfort to hurting people by sharing biblical truth about how to abide in Jesus Christ, live according to God's Word, walk in freedom, and—as a result—experience abundant life. A university professor for more than 25 years, Tina has helped many women navigate the minefields of darkness until they arrive at a place of light, hope, freedom, and joy. She is the author of numerous journal articles and books, including *Hope Beyond Loss* and *Hope Beyond Homicide*. She and her husband, Laird Jones, live in Jackson, TN, with their children.

Dr. Elacqua is available for speaking events. Contact her at TinaElacqua@letu.edu or through the Doral Cove Ministries website.

Dr. Vicki Sheafer received her B.S. in psychology and sociology from Union College in Barbourville, KY, and her M.A. and Ph.D. in Social Psychology from Miami University in Oxford, Ohio. She is currently Dean of the School of Psychology & Counseling and Professor of Psychology at LeTourneau University in Longview, TX. Her research interests revolve around the scholarship of teaching and learning in psychology, specifically digital storytelling, service learning, and the use of social media in the classroom. She has many publications and presentations on her CV. She has also been involved in several interdisciplinary research projects and government grants (SAMHSA, NSF). She is the Principal Investigator for the Wheels Project, which studies wheelchair function for people with disabilities in low-income settings. The goal is to improve the lives of people with disabilities by providing feedback to wheelchair manufacturers specializing in low-resource settings.

Lisa Guest graduated magna cum laude and Phi Beta Kappa from the University of California, Irvine, with a B.A. in English, and she completed her master's degree in medieval literature at UCLA. Through the years, Lisa has written 365-day devotionals and video curricula (script, leader's guide, participant's guide) as well as worship journal articles, book reviews, a magazine cover story, and back cover/catalog copy. She has copyedited and developed companion study guides for the work of some of today's most respected Christian writers. Her involvement in the publishing industry combines her love for the written word, her English teacher's eye for errors, and her heart for ministry. Lisa lives in Southern California with her husband, Mike, and they have three adult children.

MORE CHRISTIAN RESOURCES BY DR. ELACQUA

Dr. Tina Elacqua has been a part of the following Christian devotional books that may interest you. They are available through Amazon https://amazon.com/author/drtelacqua and Tina's website at http://www.doralcove.com

Beauty Is Soul Deep: 180 Devotions for Growing a Meaningful Inner Life
Hope Beyond Loss
Hope Beyond Homicide: Remembrance Devotionals
Shared Encouragement: Inspiration for a Woman's Soul
Today, God Wants You to Know (also available in Spanish)
365 Devotional Readings for Wives: To Love and to Cherish
365 Daily Whispers of Wisdom for Busy Women
365 Daily Whispers of Wisdom for Mothers of Preschoolers

Printed in the United States
By Bookmasters